Contents

Abbreviations

BSI	*Burma: the struggle for independence, 1944-1948* ed. H.Tinker et al. (2 vols., London, 1983-84)
IOLR	India Office Library and Records, British Library
Jinnah papers	*Jinnah papers* ed. Z.H.Zaidi (1st Series, 2 (*Pakistan in The Making 3 June-30 June 1947* (Islamabad, 1994))
PRO	Public Record Office
Transfer of Power	*The Transfer of Power* ed. N.Mansergh and P.Moon (12 vols., London, 1970-83)
USL	University of Southampton Library, MS 62: Broadlands Archives, including the Mountbatten papers

MOUNTBATTEN ON THE RECORD

EDITED BY

C.M.WOOLGAR

TO BE
DISPOSED
BY
AUTHORITY

HARTLEY INSTITUTE

UNIVERSITY OF SOUTHAMPTON

1997

ISBN 085432 643 X
(c) Contributors, 1997

Preface

This volume contains the fruits of a seminar on 'Mountbatten on the Record', sponsored by the Hartley Institute and held at the University of Southampton's conference centre at Chilworth Manor in April 1996. The aim of the seminar was to offer a view of Lord Mountbatten's career in the period 1942-8, based on the experience of participants in the events, and of recent academic research, particularly, but not exclusively, founded on Lord Mountbatten's papers in the Hartley Library at the University of Southampton.

As editor, I am grateful to my colleague, Jane Davy, for assistance with the proofs; and to Christine Ninness, for keyboarding some of the contributions.

C.M.Woolgar

Southampton
July 1997

CHAPTER 1

Mountbatten: the Triple Assignment, 1942-1948. A Recorder's Reflections
Alan Campbell-Johnson CIE, OBE, Hon. DLitt

It is a privilege I deeply value to be allowed to provide the opening contribution to this seminar held under the auspices of the Hartley Institute so early in its academic life. I address you not as a stranger but as an old friend whose links with the University of Southampton go back forty years to the launching of the Fawley Foundation Lecture and includes such support and encouragement as I could provide for the formidable Mountbatten archives to be transferred on loan from Broadlands to residence in the Hartley Library which could do full justice to them for posterity. The further inclusion of the Palmerston and Shaftesbury papers from the same source, joining those covering the Duke of Wellington's whole career, has in the course of a very few years turned Southampton University's Hartley Library from a venture with exciting possibilities into one of the most important and authoritative sources for the political, military and social history of Britain in the nineteenth and twentieth centuries. The level, range and volume of the documents housed here vindicates that claim; and historians from all over the world can be expected to explore and raid the riches of this treasure house.

It is now possible to envisage from the Hartley Institute a long sequence of seminars providing background commentary upon, and context for, the massive material housed here. It is timely that the Mountbatten papers should be given such early treatment. Indeed for this participant who, I believe, is the last surviving member of Mountbatten's staff at all three of the Headquarters of the Chief of Combined Operations, Supreme Allied Commander South-East Asia and Viceroy of India — only just in time! Already we are approaching the last of the fiftieth anniversary celebrations and there is an overdue need to refresh our memories with some glimpses at what history looked like when it was actually being made without the benefit — and I sometimes think the burden — of hindsight.

Does having survived this long cause me substantially to revise my perception of events which, both officially and unofficially, I described or placed on record at the time in my successive mutations from Air Public Relations Officer, Combined Operations Headquarters, to Officer-in-Charge of Inter-Allied Records, Headquarters Supreme Allied Commander South-East Asia, to Press Attaché to the Viceroy of India? The answer must substantially be No. The main modification or refinement which I will try this morning to develop is that I now sense that all three of Mountbatten's appointments were essentially linked; and that I now see them as, more by accident than design, stemming out of each other, and as having a common and unifying element in their basic terms of reference. They were all appointments of urgency and crisis and of growing historical significance as the world moved from a war to a post-war scenario, inevitably caught up in the problems and techniques of transferring power. Furthermore, it needs to be emphasised that a planned transference was, and remains, by no means an automatic or easy way of resolving issues of power, which is to be regarded as a neutral force whether seized or lost, and, in the last analysis, not readily to be disposed of by process of discussion and debate or by constructive and controllable action in advance of the event.

When Mountbatten was first appointed by Winston Churchill to be Adviser, and then upgraded to become Chief of Combined Operations, with a place on the British Chiefs of Staff Committee, he brought with him, as far as I am aware, no experience in handling power within a framework of specific techniques and innovations.

In considering Mountbatten's passage from orthodox naval posts to 'special duties' in Combined Operations, South-East Asia and India as essentially a single assignment in three stages, I do so in part because the duties involved led into and out of each other. In each case an unprecedented transfer of power was involved. The stakes were high and ever higher, and the time in which the response would meet the challenge was short and grew ever shorter: the downside risks were enormous. At the personal level what was needed was what Winston Churchill, with the instinct of genius, recognised in Mountbatten — a vigorous mind, hyperactive, optimistic and, above all, an officer from the outset unacquainted with defeat and defence, whose war was only for winning. All three episodes have been heavily and separately documented and subjected to critical exposure extensive enough to house a small library. Readers familiar with Philip Ziegler's massive and majestic official biography of Mountbatten will recall that those brief six years take no less than 330 of its 750 pages and 26 of its 52 chapters. Indeed, without these six momentous years he might have been expected to have provided little more than a footnote to the history of our time rather than becoming one who, in Ziegler's very last words, 'flashed brilliantly across the face of the twentieth century. The meteor is extinguished but its glow lingers on in the mind's eye.'

The *mise-en-scène* for this dramatic transformation began with the Dunkirk deliverance which, while it allowed for Britain's physical survival as a nation, marked our expulsion from the European mainland and our inability freely to return across the Channel under cover from the Royal Navy's mastery of the high seas.

With the final collapse of France, Churchill had immediately grasped the full strategic implications. Directives began pouring out of 10 Downing Street urging highest priority to be given to the design and construction of suitable landing craft. The accumulation of landing craft and supporting weaponry on a hitherto unimaginable scale would condition the length and indeed the outcome of the war. From henceforth there would need to be a new or fourth dimension of command with appropriate officers from all three services, specialists and experimenters in new techniques of warfare. A transfer of power would be involved, affecting some of the most entrenched prerogatives of the Armed Forces.

To embody and give dramatic impetus to this process, Admiral of the Fleet Sir Roger Keyes was summoned to become Director of Combined Operations. He accepted with alacrity and reacted with gusto. Four years older than Churchill himself and vastly senior to everyone else, he regarded himself as answerable only to Churchill in his capacity as Minister of Defence. He was originally lodged in the Admiralty, but it did not take him long, following some conflict with Their Lordships, to march out with his loyal band, and, crossing the road, take possession of some vacant accommodation in Richmond Terrace.

Thus turbulently was Combined Operations Headquarters born. But for all Keyes' offensive spirit, he was not able to enlarge its original remit which Bernard Fergusson in *The Watery Maze* — his memorable story of Combined Operations — defined as being 'primarily to initiate and execute raids, to interfere with German preparations for invasion and to symbolise defiance.' 'However', he added, 'when Keyes sought to stretch the bounds of his dominion to include the actual direction of all expeditions overseas, even his own most loyal and affectionate supporters realised he was sailing on the wrong course and would have to go.' When Mountbatten, extracted by Churchill from taking command of an aircraft carrier following his dramatic forays with the destroyer *Kelly*, was the surprise choice to succeed him, Fergusson claims 'the Service Ministries tended to believe that COHQ's wings had been effectively clipped. They had fought and routed an Admiral of the Fleet who was one of the Prime Minister's oldest cronies. They had little to fear from a youthful Captain in the Royal Navy. At first neither he nor the task assigned to him were taken seriously.' Mountbatten's approach to the problems of power and its transference were from the other end of the spectrum. He had on his side, Fergusson asserts, 'Youth, intelligence, imagination, enterprise and energy. His mind had not been shaped by long years in ministry moulds and he had a flare not only for new ideas of his own but still more for seeking out men who could develop these and contribute others.'

With Mountbatten's subsequent promotion from Adviser to Chief of Combined Operations, Keyes felt aggrieved that Churchill had given to his successor the status which he had refused to allow to himself — but this was not so. Mountbatten was not being authorised to supersede or overrule the Chiefs of Staff. He and his Command were being grafted on to them. Post Pearl Harbour, with America's entry into the war partnership, their role was at once enlarged — they became, informally but effectively, Joint Chiefs of Staff. Within a month of his promotion a visit of inspection to Mountbatten's Richmond Terrace Headquarters by General Marshall led to the US Chiefs of Staff sending officers of their three services to become part of Mountbatten's team. 'COHQ', in the words of Vice-Admiral Sir Ronald Brockman in his chapter on Mountbatten for the symposium *The War Lords*, 'thus became the first integrated, inter-allied, inter-service headquarters in history and the pre-runner of all that followed in the war. American units were also attached to Combined Operations for amphibious training and the strength of the Command rose to 50,000 officers and men of the three services.'

Consequent upon this historic transfer of power three formative events or developments need briefly to be recorded. First, just ten days after the Marshall visit, Mountbatten's planners and raiders brought off a brilliant coup at Saint Nazaire. Achieving a high degree of tactical surprise they injected the *Campbelltown*, a former US Lend-Lease destroyer, into the precincts of the dockyard, turning it into a block ship and filling it with explosives, then blowing it up, thus denying to the enemy for the rest of the war the only port large enough to house their formidable battleship, *Tirpitz*.

This was to be followed some five months later, however, by a spectacular failure, the raid, or so-called 'Reconnaissance in Force' on Dieppe. The ambiguities and controversies surrounding this tragic event are endless and have been recalled, mostly, but not exclusively, to Mountbatten's and COHQ's detriment. They transcend the purpose of this review which is to note the raid's impact on the larger power scene. At a critical planning stage, when he should have been presiding over the proceedings, Mountbatten was whisked away by Churchill to confer with President Roosevelt and if possible pre-empt the risk of American landing craft being diverted from Europe into higher priorities against Japan in the Pacific. Dieppe emerged as the only surviving symbol of the Allies' serious intention to open a Second Front, not now, alas, in 1942, but as soon as possible thereafter.

Disagreements on implementation concealed a far deeper divergence on where the ultimate location for the return to Europe should be. The formation at the end of 1941 of a Combined Commanders' Committee served only to sharpen the controversy, with General Sir Bernard Paget and Air Marshal Sir Sholto Douglas solidly in favour of the Pas de Calais, and Mountbatten, at considerable risk to his credibility and prospects of survival, holding out for Normandy and the Cotentin Peninsula. It is, I think, of considerable significance that Mountbatten deliberately chose to do battle on this vital issue as a Combined Commander rather than relying on his membership of the Chiefs of Staff Committee to overrule them.

Even more impressive was his initiative in organising and presiding over the special conference held aboard HMS *Warren* (an hotel and not a ship, by the way) at Largs in Scotland under the code name 'Rattle'. According to Fergusson, on whose account I rely, 'So eminent and numerous was the rank and position of those attending it, that the ribald christened it the Field of the Cloth of Gold ... Among those in attendance were 20 assorted Generals, 11 Air Marshals and Air Commodores, eight Admirals and Brigadiers galore.' Fifteen Americans were also there. In assessing the level and range of the decisions clearing away, as they did, so many doubts and misgivings, Fergusson concludes that 'In many ways "Rattle" was the summit of COHQ's achievement. It was at "Rattle" that the final lodgement area (Normandy) was approved to the full satisfaction to those who at that time looked like bearing the personal responsibility for the greatest operation ever carried out. It was', he added, 'splendidly produced, and carefully stage-managed, but there was no feeling that a confidence trick was being put across. Seven important officers sat at the high table. In the chair was Mountbatten, the youngest of them by eight years.' At 'Rattle', COHQ's prize 'strange device', the Mulberry Harbour, was at last taken on board for genuine implementation.

At one blow with the removal of the need for the real invasion to capture an established port in a built-up area, Dieppe, ironically and quite unintentionally, served to become a potent deception operation helping to provide a plausible cover for the bizarre developments of Mulberry and Pluto (Pipe-Line Under The Ocean) while encouraging the German High Command to disrupt the balance it had struck between the Atlantic Wall's perimeter and depth defences and to reinforce the former in the wrong places. 'Rattle' also confirmed the alliance between Combined Operations and the embryonic headquarters of what was to become in due course General Eisenhower's Supreme Command. By the autumn of 1943, power had been effectively transferred to Combined Operations and then from it to an integrated Supreme Command capable of exploiting to the full its unique know-how.

So, when Mountbatten himself was selected by Churchill and endorsed by Roosevelt to take charge of another Supreme

Command in South-East Asia, Combined Operations' controlling role, as a result of 'Rattle', was already past its zenith. It would, however, be a mistake to suggest that all was sweetness and light; for, as Fergusson pungently observes, 'COHQ was rooted in dislike and grew in an atmosphere of distrust. There were officers in high positions — though not in the highest — who never ceased throughout the war to resent and combat its special position. Such of their juniors as shared their prejudice looked on the denizens of COHQ as a coven of deluded druids.'

The principal sources of disaffection were within both the Admiralty and the War Office, and Mountbatten was particularly sensitive to the enmity being enlarged and defined by his acquisition as a mere substantive Captain of an unprecedented inter-service and inter-allied post carrying with it the treble acting rank of full Admiral and doing a General out of his job in the process.

Parallels with the Combined Operations assignment were immediately apparent. Total defeat — this time, at the hands of the Japanese; marginal escape and survival — this time through the jungles of Burma; the need once again for exclusively offensive action; the development of an amphibious strategy, and with it, of course, the ever-dominant requirement for landing craft. The final need was to get a move on and out of the Burma cul-de-sac. Mountbatten was once again heavily out-gunned by the rank and experience of his Service Commanders, and he had as Deputy Supreme Commander a particularly prickly colleague in General Stilwell, not so affectionately known as Vinegar Joe. Mountbatten brought out with him high hopes soon to be dashed and firm resolve soon to be tested. Within weeks after his installation as Supremo, the Americans reasserted their firm intention to give top priority to Pacific strategy for the ultimate conquest of Japan, relegating SEAC from the outset to the role of a strategic sideshow.

I have read accounts of how Mountbatten, criticised for

having been over-indulgent in accumulating staff at COHQ, then went overboard with a vast army of some 7,000 bodies in South-East Asia. This is not in accordance with the facts. He inherited special links and large established units of 11 Army Group, Eastern Fleet and an Air Command. His own Supreme Command embodied an inter-service team of under 500. However, as Brockman justly observes, 'The problem of establishing the Command structure was daunting and his subordinate Commanders-in-Chief and his Deputy would need very careful handling.'

There was from the outset a political as well as a military dimension involved. Stilwell had in fact acquired no less than four different posts at four different levels, answerable in only one of them directly to Mountbatten as Supreme Commander — the others sharing his grudging allegiance, the US Government, the US Chiefs of Staff and Generalissimo Chiang Kai-shek. It was a scenario worthy of Alice in Wonderland and the Mad Hatter's tea party.

Also at odds with the concept of a unifying Supreme Allied Commander was his operational relationship with Eastern Fleet. Here the Admiralty, while allowing the naval Commander-in-Chief to be subordinate to the Supreme Commander in all matters concerning security and support of the land campaign and amphibious operations in the theatre, insisted on his remaining answerable to Their Lordships for wider operations in regard to the security of sea communications and with offensive action at sea against the enemy. Mountbatten at the time of his appointment had protested in vain to the First Sea Lord (Dudley Pound) against this built-in ambiguity. Fortunately the goodwill of the successive Eastern Fleet Commanders, Admirals Fraser and Power, provided the good sense that had been missing.

Equally ambivalent was the relationship with India Command as far as land forces were concerned. Here, bearing in mind how heavily dependent South-East Asia Command would be on Indian troops to sustain our operational capability in Burma and beyond, the British Government, in Brockman's words, 'decided it was constitutionally impracticable to place troops in India under a commander not responsible to the Government of India. They further considered the two Commands were too large for one man to manage effectively. SEAC therefore retained control of operations and India became the base of all three Services, both Commands remaining equal.' It must however have been particularly galling for an officer of General Auckinleck's stature and battle experience to find his operational powers taken away from his grasp to be handed over to a naval Captain acting Admiral, and it might well have been what Brockman called 'an unworkable proposition' but for Auckinleck's magnanimity and Mountbatten's tact engendering again the necessary goodwill.

It was, however, in the deployment of the Air Force within his Command that, to quote Brockman again, 'It may unquestionably be said that Mountbatten made one of his greatest contributions to the success of the South-East Asia campaign. He was so dissatisfied with the separate control of British and US Air Forces that on 11 December 1943, he issued a directive of great political consequence. He turned the British Air Commander-in-Chief into the Allied Air Commander-in-Chief with all Air Forces under him. He grouped the RAF and US Army Air Force in Burma into a single integrated force under the US Air General (General Stratemeyer). Great improvement in morale and efficiency resulted.'

This was indeed a crucial transfer of power and it was made only just in time. The forcing-house in Burma was provided by the Japanese themselves, first in the Arakan and then on a far bigger scale in the Imphal area to the North, when they developed flanking attacks in the expectation of defending forces having to retreat back on their supply lines; but the order came this time to stand firm and await supply, which duly arrived, from the air. This *coup de main* was only achieved by Mountbatten twice in close succession taking it upon himself to divert American transport aircraft from their regular supply missions to China over the Himalayan hump and, in the process, directly disobeying President Roosevelt's clear order not to do so the first time, and certainly not again. With the unauthorised backing of 30 US transport aircraft, two whole divisions were moved from the Arakan to the central front, there to lay the foundations for General Slim's and his Fourteenth Army's historic break-out and ultimate break-through, to Rangoon. The entire operation was rendered possible throughout only by Anglo-American air support of heroic proportions and at high risk maintained at double the recommended sustained rate not just over a few days, but over months on end.

The same propensity for applying original priorities at Combined Operations now served to provide crucial backing for Slim's brilliant direction of the Fourteenth Army and its reconquest of Burma. From the outset Mountbatten recognised the combined impact of malaria and the monsoon as being more deadly and debilitating than the fanatical Japanese themselves. By setting up a high-level specialist medical team with experts in tropical diseases, he was able to reduce the ratio of sickness to battle casualties from a crippling 120 to 1 to a feasible 10 to 1, thereby making good what had seemed to be at the outset a vain boast on his part to continue the campaign without interruption throughout the monsoon. Such initiatives are the true ingredients of victory in war. Slim in his greatness had no doubt. 'We did it together', he said.

But with the sudden collapse of Japan following upon the nuclear bombing of Hiroshima and Nagasaki, South-East Asia — a strategic sideshow in war — covering an area as large as Europe, encompassing a population of over 120 million, was suddenly caught up in a vast power vacuum liable to be filled up at any moment by violent and anarchic forces. Mountbatten, at Potsdam, found himself the recipient of a huge new segment to his Command — the whole of Indonesia, no less. The complexities of transferring power were deepened and magnified beyond what any normal guidelines could be expected to quantify. Mountbatten's annexe to his Despatches, entitled *Post Surrender Tasks* (which was not authorised to be published for many years after the war), does its best to soften the impact of the drama which he was to confront. It became abundantly clear that four years of Japanese occupation was in itself a species of time bomb, and created an environment which could not accept a simple restoration of pre-war power for all these high officials locked away in cold storage and waiting, as of right, to be set up again in the seats of imperial authority from which they had been so rudely ejected.

In the welter of conflicting claims and obligations, Mountbatten moved his Command Headquarters from Kandy to Singapore to be somewhat nearer the centre of the action. Finding himself by a sudden transmutation in effect the Military Governor of the whole of South-East Asia, he was called upon simultaneously to cope with the power claims of Aung San and his nationalist guerrillas in Burma; with embryonic Communist agitation in Malaya and Singapore; with Indo-China arbitrarily partitioned at the Sixteenth Parallel — French Gaullist versus Vichyite to the South of it, Chiang Kai-shek's bailiwick to the North, and with Ho Chi Minh lurking somewhere in the wings, in due course to supersede the lot; with Indonesia containing Soekarno firmly installed by a large undefeated Japanese army, and the Dutch automatically expecting to be re-installed and to replace him; and with Thailand, technically an enemy defeated in a war which it had not been called upon to fight, but now summoned to sign a peace treaty, thereby releasing its rich rice granary to help stave off the threats of starvation throughout the whole area.

Superimposed on all this was the desperate problem of repatriating a vast army of Allied prisoners of war, in which process Lady Mountbatten, invested with Red Cross and St John's authority, herself earned fame and provided heroic support.

Everywhere the central problem was how to transfer sustainable power which extended Mountbatten's military remit farther than could ever have been envisaged into political arenas, and as such was a baptism by total immersion. Brockman who as his Naval Secretary was at his side from South-East Asia days onwards in all his various posts for 20 years and was in a unique position to assess his Chief's overall performance, speaks of these accumulated post-surrender responsibilities bringing with them 'daunting political and administrative problems. He faced and tackled them with his characteristic self-confidence, vigour and clarity of mind, supported by a wise liberal attitude which set a tone for future relations with the population of colonial territories.'

I was privileged to be a colleague of Brockman on Mountbatten's staff both in South-East Asia and India and I wholeheartedly endorse his judgement. However, lacking the admirable professional reserve of the silent service, my reactions went a little further. In a profile published in the magazine *Encounter* at the time of the publication of Ziegler's official biography in 1985, I wrote, 'If ever a man was grappling in darkness with destiny that was Mountbatten in South-East Asia from the autumn of 1945 to the spring of 1946. Lord Blake's attribution of "genius" certainly applies to his performance during this frenetic period. I detected, when all this pressure was on, Mountbatten's instinctive sense of the nature of power and his no less instinctive sense of timing to meet its demands. His flair was in his skill in applying communications (public and private) to assuage their harsher realities. When out of the blue he learned that he was to be the last Viceroy, he was already an authority on the transfer of power, having assumed it at Combined Operations and remitted it in South-East Asia.'

So, I reach belatedly, but not, I hope, irrelevantly, the climax of Mountbatten's involvement with transferring power — his appointment by the Prime Minister, Mr Attlee, and the Labour

Government, after the briefest of vacations and return to naval duties, to replace Lord Wavell, and to become the last Viceroy of India. While I do not expect many of you have read the daily account of my experiences in the post of first and last Press Attaché to a Viceroy, you will not expect me to take you through or analyse in detail this historic transaction. It has been the subject of extensive critical study of widely varying range and quality over the years, and in any case you will shortly have the benefit of Dr Talbot addressing himself exclusively to the subject.

It will meet my purpose here if I concentrate on what I regard as the central issue of this address — that by becoming Viceroy of India in 1947 he was returning, but on a larger and more momentous scale, to what was essentially the same assignment that he had been called upon to undertake at Combined Operations and South-East Asia. Towards the end of his life he was under constant pressure to provide enterprising authors and journalists with 'The Inside Story' of his real part in the attainment of India's and Pakistan's independence. Equally he was at pains to retail his version of events on television within the twelve part documentary, *The Life and Times of Lord Mountbatten*. But the outcome has not, frankly, been entirely successful, has tended to induce rather more heat than light, and, at times, to trivialise and distort issues. In a long correspondence he had with me over the years, Mountbatten from time to time would ask it I could throw a little of the latter on some given point of contention.

This led me in a letter dated 6 October 1975 to react in some depth to a memorandum he was preparing — namely to answer the question, 'Was the speed of transfer responsible for massacres?' In it I submitted to him the following analysis which, 21 years later, I feel justified in incorporating into this address, for it represents a perspective to which I still firmly adhere. I wrote as follows:

'What I am still in doubt about is the form and emphasis of the question to which the memo addresses itself. To stay with the question as worded — "Was speed of transfer responsible for massacres?" — distorts and narrows the perspective and puts you in a far more defensive posture than is either desirable or necessary. The question that in historical terms needs consideration — even though it is hypothetical — is what kind of a holocaust would we have been dealing with if there had been no political settlement and a mere demission to whomsoever might have seen fit to appoint themselves as our successors at the terminal date of June 30th 1948? Wavell's alternative solution upon which you needed to improve was a phased military withdrawal — no more, no less. In the light of our experience the consequences of that do not bear thinking about.

My advice would be to continue to uphold the case for the speed of transfer within the framework of three sets of wise words attributable to Ismay, Rajagopalachari and Lloyd George, for they do help to put the issue in its full perspective:

1. Ismay's comment upon your becoming Viceroy was that it was "like taking command of a ship in mid-ocean with fire on the decks and ammunition in the hold". He said this to illustrate his thesis that India in March 1947 provided the most dangerous situation affecting the civil order that he had ever seen anywhere in peacetime. Lawlessness, riots and bloodshed had, as your memo shows, already escalated to this point well

in advance of our arrival on the scene. With political uncertainty and the run down of the civil authority, the communal crisis had gained enough hold to constitute an immediate revolutionary threat to the entire Sub-Continent. I would quote here from your Viceroyalty Report for the period of 22nd March - 15th April. "By the end of my first week in office it had, indeed, become apparent that I would find the beginnings of an extensive civil war on my hands unless quick action were taken. It was becoming clear that an early decision was the only way of converting Indian minds from their present emotionalism to stark realism and of countering the spread of strife, but at that stage there appeared to be little common ground on which to build any agreed solution for the future of India."

2. It was this sombre context which gave such force to the dictum of Rajagopalachari that "If you had not transferred power when you did, there would have been no power to transfer." It cannot be too strongly stressed that by March 1947 political negotiations had been going on virtually without a break and at the highest level for over two years. Although the various plans had proved abortive, the parties and personalities involved had come sufficiently near to success for great expectations to have been aroused and with failure for corresponding tension and frustration to have been induced. In this context, June 1948 was indeed the end of the road; for any solution based upon the leaders' consent and readiness to compromise within that deadline was, by definition, to forestall the prospects of anarchy

and to allow more time for successor governments to stave it off. The scale and intensity of the Punjab tragedy has perhaps stood in the way of this point being properly appreciated, but as you have rightly pointed out, 97% of India's population was unaffected and enjoyed the maximum administrative continuity when the time came for us to go.

3. This leads me to recall Lloyd George's wise words that "You cannot leap across a precipice in two jumps." This is precisely what those who wanted to delay and mitigate the process by putting administrative preconditions to the transfer of political power were trying to do. R.A.Butler is perhaps the most important exponent of this point of view. He aptly called his autobiography *The Art of the Possible.* He would, I am convinced, have been hard put to it to reconcile that principle with keeping the Interim Government in being a day longer than you did; and if you had not given top priority to a political settlement, you would have been reduced to Section 93 rule within hours of taking over and, with due respect to Rab, that would have been practising the "Art of the Impossible".'

In short, Mountbatten's Viceroyalty was the end of an end-game which had been conducted for not just two, but five years, by the same players familiar with every move and counter-move. All the principal personalities, men of high calibre, were lawyers skilled in the arts of special pleading; but within that framework they had indeed become 'senior citizens' whose experiences of actual power had been confined to agitation. Of all the leaders, the one who set the highest priority to changing his role of agitator and becoming an administrator, was Vallabhbhai Patel.

While Mountbatten was strictly an amateur when it came to political dialectic, he revelled in verbal argument and debate, and by the time he reached Delhi he had become highly skilled at it. Recognition that time was running out was mutual on all sides. Once agreement was reached Mountbatten did not rush events, events rushed Mountbatten. Immediately after the leaders had accepted the Partition formula, Mountbatten presented them with a paper entitled 'The Administrative Consequences of Partition' which all concerned found no difficulty in handing down to three trusted subordinates, one of whom had actually written the document, and who in their turn found it relatively easy to clear up points of contention.

The role of the Interim Government, set up after the breakdown of the Cabinet Mission Plan, was at an end and it effectively disintegrated. The biggest danger throughout was the possibility that one or other of the leaders would renege and relapse into the policy of negation and denial, from which veto all the parties would be the losers. Mountbatten was well aware of this traumatic risk and it conditioned his attitude to the problem throughout.

It was just such a context that led Woodrow Wyatt when reviewing my book, *Mission with Mountbatten*, 44 years ago, to reach a surprising but, I believe, valid conclusion. Wyatt as a young Labour MP had in 1946 been personal assistant to Sir Stafford Cripps in his capacity as member of the Cabinet Mission, the British Government's last abortive attempt to achieve united Indian independence, and was well placed to assess the key personalities, issues and motives involved. Having paid tribute to Mountbatten's charm and energy without which he could never have persuaded Congress and Jinnah to accept what they largely disapproved of, Wyatt went on to say, 'His only failure was Jinnah, who thawed less under Mountbatten's extrovert friendliness than anyone else and who was disliked by the Viceroy; but Mountbatten's dislike of Jinnah made him anxious to be fair to the Moslem League, so that on balance they gained slightly more than they would have done if Mountbatten and Jinnah had been as friendly as Mountbatten and Nehru.'

When Jinnah, after allowing Mountbatten to believe that a temporary joint Indo-Pakistan Governor Generalship might serve Pakistan's interest, finally rejected the idea and came down in favour of himself, Mountbatten had to face up to a real crisis. Lady Mountbatten, who well knew how far it was wise or appropriate to pressurise her husband, urged him to leave and not stay on after 15 August on the grounds that he would have lost his impartial status. After much anxious soul-searching and double checking, in which I myself was quite heavily involved, he finally accepted the clear majority view of his staff that it was his duty to accept the unique and unconditional honour offered him by India, and that at both national and international level the best interests not only of India, but also of both Britain and Pakistan, would be served by his doing so. In propagandist and polemical terms a high price had to be paid — the risk was inevitable but acceptable. He stayed on to share in the ordeals that lay ahead, and in doing so made a continuing and invaluable contribution in support of a successor leadership facing the critical immediate aftermath of the transfer of power.

So what of the man himself? After six years in close proximity and watching him in action on an almost daily basis, I was fascinated by the scale of paradox that went to make up his personality. He was the radical royalist, the innocent in-fighter, the loquacious listener, the generalist in love with detail, candid but elusive, a razor-sharp intellect but not a conceptual thinker, interested in the 'how' rather than the 'why', obsessional but objective, passionate but unprejudiced, bold but canny, the cunning good man. Rajagopalachari stressed his charm, not always an unqualified compliment these days, but in C.R.'s case spelt out by him as meaning 'a quality of the heart'.

When it came to handling the triple assignment, the meaning of the mix was the potency of his instinct, which told him that in the particular transfers of power to which he had been committed, the deepest danger rested in delay. So the title he accepted for his book of speeches delivered as last Viceroy of India contained his victorious response — it was simply *Time Only to Look Forward*.

CHAPTER 2

Mountbatten at South-East Asia Command
Nicholas Owen
The Queen's College, Oxford

One of the paradoxes of the decolonisation of the European colonial empires in the years after the Second World War was that, even in its demise, the imperial state often felt obliged to make greater use of repression and pacification than it had needed to do since the stage of conquest. At a time when the anti-colonial agencies of the United Nations and the superpowers exposed the activities of colonial powers to a harsher scrutiny and criticism than before, they undertook both short and violent police actions and lengthy colonial emergencies, dedicating what seem in retrospect considerable resources to the task of meeting the challenge of militant and confident nationalist movements and turning them in more acceptable directions.[1]

It was the military arm of the imperial state that felt this dilemma most acutely. Loss of empire challenged the interests and self-esteem of soldiers, especially where it entailed political surrender to their military opponents. Orders from the metropole were often ambiguous. Winning the hearts and minds of colonial populations dragged soldiers into political activities for which they had generally received little training. Public relations often required that military activities be covert, even disowned, and at no time was there an absence of metropolitan critics squeamish about the use of repression. Colonial engagements usually consisted not of set battles but of guerrilla warfare, characterised by uncertainties about who the enemy was and even how to tell when it had been defeated. *In extremis*, the military could take matters into their own hands in a public act of revolt, as occurred most famously in Algeria and in the Portuguese empire in southern Africa. But even where there were no overt acts of defiance, the privately stated views of military leaders inevitably influenced the calculations of their political masters.

The purpose of the present article is to analyse some of these themes through exploration of the contribution and ideas of Louis Mountbatten. Mountbatten's career intersects with that of British imperial decline at a number of points. Most famously, he was, of course, the last Viceroy and architect of the partition of India. His appointment to that post had been largely the result of his handling of the resurgent nationalist movements of South-East Asia during his time as Supreme Commander at SEAC. After its completion, he returned to the Navy, rising to Commander-in-Chief of the Mediterranean, in which capacity he encountered the struggle for *enosis* in Cyprus, and more directly, Dom Mintoff's pursuit of Maltese independence. As First Sea Lord, he clashed with Anthony Eden over the political unwisdom of the Suez expedition of October 1956. As Chief of the Defence Staff, it fell to him to handle the reorganisation of Britain's defences, with its profound implications for Britain's ability to intervene in post-imperial crises east of Suez.

Such extensive involvement in these momentous events has, of course, made Mountbatten a highly controversial figure in the history of decolonisation. Taken at his own estimation, his leadership was decisive in ensuring that British decolonisation was characterised by judicious and well-planned efficiency. In planning his own funeral, Mountbatten left instructions that if the Prime Minister should wish to say a few words, they should say that 'his personal leadership, as long ago as 1945, had set the line on which the British Empire changed itself into the Commonwealth of sovereign states'.[2] Needless to say, this rosy picture has been greeted with considerable scepticism, especially among Conservatives, many of whom among Mountbatten's contemporaries regarded him as a baleful and destructive influence responsible for hasty, ill-considered and treacherous scuttles, and whose criticisms have recently been given a fresh airing by the historian, Andrew Roberts.[3] These two perspectives share one common feature: they both take it as axiomatic that Mountbatten's part in the history of decolonisation was decisive, whether for good or ill. The purpose of this paper is to test this assumption against the evidence of Mountbatten's time at South-East Asia Command (SEAC). I begin by tracing the development of Mountbatten's ideas on anti-colonial nationalism in the re-occupation of Ceylon, Burma and Malaya. In the second half of the paper, in examining the role of SEAC in the reoccupation of French Indo-China and Dutch Indonesia, I aim to place Mountbatten's contribution in a comparative perspective. My conclusion is that Mountbatten's ideas, though significant, owed a good deal to a set of peculiar circumstances that not all military leaders have enjoyed.

I

Mountbatten's mind seems to have turned to consideration of the political implications of his command at an early stage. Only three weeks after appointment as Supreme Commander, he was discussing the political future of Burma with the Governor, Reginald Dorman-Smith. 'I must say I found the Supreme Commander displayed a very keen interest in the political aspect of his future task', noted the Governor. Mountbatten stressed the need to meet Burma's political aspirations through a statement of constitutional advance, and not simply to hand Burma back to 'European rule and to the British and Indian business interests'. He feared, presciently, that officials would not be welcomed back as they had fled and left the Burmese in the lurch. Dorman-Smith, who regarded the Burmese people as naturally disloyal and possessed of 'the cunning and shrewdness of the eternal peasant', thought the Burmese mind did not work this way.[4] Of course, Mountbatten did not envisage a rapid transfer of power in Burma. Rather, he seems to have favoured a more full-blooded paternalism. In August 1944, as the Japanese began their retreat, he was thinking in terms not of political pronouncements but of an announcement of social and economic policy with the purpose of safeguarding the Burmese rural population from 'outside exploitation and in particular Indian money-lenders', for the Japanese invasion had fortuitously lifted a large burden of debt from the shoulders of the Burmese peasantry and made them supporters of independence.[5]

Shortly after transferring his headquarters from Delhi to Kandy in April 1944, Mountbatten faced the first indication of the need to accommodate Asian nationalism. In February 1944, the Ceylonese Board of Ministers had produced a plan for constitutional advance. The proposals were unacceptable to the Colonial Office in London, which had insisted that consideration of such questions must wait until the war was over. Mountbatten, in alliance with the Ceylonese Governor and the local Commander-in-Chief, forced a retreat, arguing that unless a Commission were appointed to consider the plan, elections would have to be held which would be likely to jeopardise Ceylon's role as an operational base and source of vital natural rubber supplies.[6] The experiences of Allied troops landing in Italy in the first half of 1944 and the subsequent invasion of northern France also demonstrated that, in order to achieve its military objectives, SEAC would have to win the co-operation of local populations. This seems to have reinforced Mountbatten's determination to deploy political as well as military force. In September 1944, he told the Colonial Secretary, Oliver Stanley, that 'the example of what the helpful attitudes of the local populations in Italy and France has meant to our fighting forces makes me apprehensive at the thought that we may be neglecting to procure for ourselves a weapon which may not be as potent as in the European countries occupied by the Nazis, but which it seems to me that it would be folly to underestimate.'[7]

As British troops moved to re-occupy Burma, Mountbatten

accordingly followed a policy of liberal treatment. He ruled out whipping of offenders and the use of death sentences for illicit possession of arms.[8] More controversial, however, was his decision to recognise and re-arm the Anti-Fascist Organisation (AFO) of Aung San. Aung San was leader of the Burma National Army (BNA), established by the Japanese in 1942, but which had switched sides as its sponsors suffered military defeat and failed to deliver their initial promises. Force 136, the Far Eastern arm of the Special Operations Executive, favoured the offer of arms largely on the grounds, as one of their official historians puts it, that where there were rival nationalist groups, SOE 'tended to back the one that showed the most promise of throwing the enemy out fast'.[9] Naturally, such a pragmatic attitude offended the Burmese Civil Affairs Officers, many of whom came from the colonial administration anxious to preserve its pre-war network of Burmese allies and loyalists. Many of these, especially the Karens, Kachins and Chins (the hill tribes), were rightly fearful of the ambitions of Aung San.[10] To re-arm the BNA would mean granting a powerful voice in the post-war constitutional order to the Anti-Fascist Peoples Freedom League (AFPFL) whose *Thakin* members the administrators had spent the pre-war years locking up.[11] Its anti-fascist credentials were doubted. It was, the Civil Affairs Officers insisted, not pro-British, or even anti-Japanese, but simply pro-Burman, and unrepresentative at that.[12] The Deputy Governor, Sir John Wise, thought its leaders 'unstable and treacherous and their political consciousness ... of the crudest'.[13] For Brigadier Prescott — Deputy Director of Civil Affairs — they were 'not patriots, such as were the Maquis in France', but 'disgruntled elements who have backed the wrong horse and who are endeavouring to cover their bets'.[14]

Thus advised by his Civil Affairs staff, the Burmese Commander-in-Chief, Sir Oliver Leese, rejected the request of Force 136. Its commander, Colin Mackenzie, thereupon went over his head to Mountbatten, who promptly overruled Leese, insisting that the advice of the Civil Affairs Officers '[did] not fit into the broad policy for Burma that I have decided upon'.[15] Indeed, Mountbatten clearly intended that Aung San should be recognised as a national leader even once it became apparent that the rapid collapse of the Japanese Army had made his military support less valuable. Mountbatten blocked attempts by Burmese Civil Affairs Officers to charge Aung San with war crimes,[16] worked hard to incorporate his forces into the Burmese Army and asked Dorman-Smith to provide a guarantee that his representatives would be included in the advisory council that was to be set up when civil government was restored. Dorman-Smith and the War Cabinet's India Committee strongly opposed the 'semblance of recognition' this would imply.[17] The BNA was a political army, and building it up was certain to change decisively the agenda of Burmese politics. It was agreed that Dorman-Smith would meet a range of Burmese politicians, to include representatives of the AFO. However, while Mountbatten maintained to the Civil Affairs staff that Dorman-Smith would meet 'prominent politicians representing all shades of opinion',[18] he believed that the BNA were the only ones who mattered. He was, according to a note in his diary, 'completely on their side'.[19] Britain's traditional allies were 'non-entities'. Had they been otherwise they would have emerged within a few hours of the British arrival in Rangoon. It was only 'these politically active elements who brought the BNA over to our side' whose grievances should be addressed. 'They', Mountbatten insisted, 'are the potential trouble-makers, and it is only by dealing with them ... successfully, that the Governor can achieve anything at this meeting which could justify my having allowed him to hold it.'[20]

Mountbatten's decision caused some consternation in London. To build up Aung San's forces as national liberators or take them as spokespersons for the Burmese would be dangerous and contrary to Britain's long term interests. On this point, Mountbatten was opposed by numbers of the Civil Affairs Officers, the Chiefs of Staff and the War Cabinet, including the Labour members. Indeed, according to the Counsellor to the Governor of Burma, the War Cabinet's instructions about treading carefully with Aung San were 'erod[ed] ... almost to the point of nullification'.[21]

Why did Mountbatten insist on recognising Aung San's BNA? There were good operational reasons for doing so. As Mackenzie pointed out, it was scarcely practical to prevent Aung San's followers from re-arming themselves anyway, with the discarded or confiscated or stolen weapons of the Japanese. But Mountbatten's championing of Aung San went further than the grim recognition of British impotence. What seems to have convinced him was the activism of the BNA. There was a danger, he acknowledged to the Chiefs of Staff, that recognition would offend the 'more respectable elements of the population'. But 'it must be remembered that the more respectable elements have been inactive while the elements who are about to undertake this action comprise the active, politically conscious and organised elements in the country — those who are in fact in position to give trouble or not to give it depending on our present decision.' To re-arm them was no different from the treatment given to European resistance movements in Italy, Rumania, Hungary and Finland.[22]

The problem with the strategy was its implications for what the Cabinet Committee had termed the 'less active but more dependable elements'.[23] Doubtless too the claims of the other Burmese groups were much exaggerated and even Dorman-Smith was forced to acknowledge wartime defeats had undermined their credibility. That Dorman-Smith and his fellow administrators felt obliged to repay them owed a good deal to the loyalties they felt for former allies and to the circumstances of their departure in 1942, sentiments which Mountbatten, as a newcomer to the region, could not be expected to share. If he seemed less concerned about the need to repay old debts, it was partly because he had not incurred them. But the *Thakin* party, from which Aung San drew most of his followers, had received relatively little popular support before the war, and one may seriously doubt the claim of Colin Mackenzie that it represented the 'only organisation of politically educated Plains Burmese'.[24] On any view except the operational, Sir John Wise claimed, the only hope of ordered progress to Burmese self-government lay with the respectable elements which had been inactive under Japanese rule, but did not willingly acquiesce in it.[25]

The dispute between Mountbatten and the Civil Affairs Officers should not be regarded as a clash between Blimpish die-hards and liberals. It was in essence one about the correct approach to be taken to an unprecedented and tricky task: the re-occupation of former colonial territories, after ignominious military defeat, at a time when the Japanese remained undefeated and the fundamental purposes of colonial policy were being questioned as never before. For some, the best method of reinforcing British power was an initial show of force, before political negotiations were started.[26] 'We must impress upon local inhabitants', wrote Esler Dening, Mountbatten's political adviser, 'that we are now possessed of force and organisation which were so conspicuously lacking at the time of our defeat ... Politically it is vitally important that our return to territories occupied for so long by Japanese should take place in a manner most calculated to impress the inhabitants with the security we are capable of providing.'[27] Underlying this view was the belief that colonial peoples respected force. 'Leniency in the East', argued Philip Joubert, 'is always regarded as an indication of weakness.'[28]

The advantages of such a course of action were that it enabled the incoming colonial administration to negotiate from a position of strength. Moderates whose nationalist ambitions were held to be compatible with the preservation of metropolitan interests could be won over through the offer of political concessions and radicals forced to the negotiating table. This technique — the so-called *tâche d'huile* — was successfully adopted both by Leclerc in

Indo-China after the departure of SEAC, and by Templar during the Malayan Emergency. Indeed Mountbatten himself seems to have seen the force of these arguments when he concluded in October 1944 that any political appeal to the Burmese should wait until after reconquest, because it would not be until that stage that Britain would be in any position to implement any promise given.[29]

However, the disadvantages were equally apparent. Repression was expensive, especially when military resources were tightly stretched as demobilisation was accelerated in the wake of Japanese surrender. It threatened to exacerbate anti-British feeling and expose her politicians to diplomatic and domestic criticism from those who believed that the war had been fought for, among other things, the rights of self-determination of small states. Given Britain's need for diplomatic and economic support from the United States, and the dependence of his forces upon American Lend-Lease equipment, Mountbatten had to ensure that SEAC did not live down to its nickname (Save England's Asian Colonies). Moreover, SEAC was heavily dependent on Indian troops which, as Auchinleck pointed out, could only be used to police former colonies at the risk of antagonising Indian political opinion.[30]

The other model of colonial re-occupation reversed the stages. It consisted of getting ahead of the nationalists, in granting political concessions before they became unavoidable, thereby keeping the initiative, sustaining the moderates and undercutting the ability of radicals to argue the redundancy of the British connection. The most-quoted example of such a policy was the stance taken by the Liberal Government towards South Africa after the Boer War, which Mountbatten held had transformed rebels such as Smuts and Botha into patriots.[31] Such a strategy depended, however, upon two prerequisites. First, a clear distinction had to be made between moderates and radicals, a diagnosis that newly arrived soldiers working with out-of-date political intelligence were not in a good position to make. Secondly, to retain the initiative, it was vital that the occupying forces retain a near-monopoly of the use of force. Once armed, nationalist groups were bound to use their new-found strength to dominate their own communities and to present the British with the prospect of departure or a drawn-out civil war.[32]

The Cabinet and those of the senior officers at SEAC who — unlike Mountbatten — had served in the Mediterranean theatre were fearful of the consequences of re-arming Aung San because they were well aware of the problems that had arisen from the employment of Greek anti-fascist partisans of EAM and ELAS.[33] Mountbatten seems to have felt few reservations. Aung San and his colleagues, he insisted to the Civil Affairs Officers, were 'indisputably an organised political party' and not a 'federation of murder gangs'.[34]

At all events, it is hard not to conclude that Mountbatten's strategy was at best only a partial success.[35] Given the rapid collapse of the Japanese forces, the value of the BNA as a military ally had proved less significant than Mountbatten had been led to believe by Mackenzie, a fact he was forced to acknowledge in a late attempt to cut it down to size. Indeed, the vast bulk of Aung San's forces were never absorbed into the Burmese Army, for Aung San proved unwilling, or unable, to make so great a concession to the occupying forces. Nor, despite the hopes of Force 136, did it prove possible to recover the arms distributed to them. Rather the BNA, or the Patriotic Burma Forces (PBF), as it was renamed, was deployed as a political army. The AFPFL was keen to exploit the temporary advantage that wartime dislocations had given it to silence its political opponents and raise campaign funds, often by means of pressure and extortion.[36] Almost all local crime, Donnison reported, could be traced to the ex-guerrillas sponsored by the BNA.[37] Within the Civil Service, a number of Civil Affairs Officers had claimed that 'the general run of the population in rural Lower Burma are terrified of the PBF' and that the general run of government officials were afraid to co-operate with the British for fear of its reprisals.[38] Lindop, the Deputy Chief of Civil Affairs with the Fourteenth Army, reported that many Burmese villagers thought the BNA worse than the Japanese, and were highly critical of the British for sponsoring it. Most favoured the installation of an administration dedicated to post-war reconstruction and the postponement of political discussions until after fresh elections had been held.[39]

Thus although Mountbatten had hoped to see the AFPFL break into a number of parties as the defeat of the Japanese and the announcement of political concessions took the wind from its sails, it simply grew in strength. At no stage of the negotiations with Dorman-Smith did it adjust or moderate its demands, unchanged from those it had presented to the Japanese. Undoubtedly, Aung San's movement enjoyed great popularity for its belated, but genuine defiance of the Japanese.[40] But it was also strengthened by the fact that its leaders were in high level negotiations with Mountbatten. As Wise noted bitterly, Aung San 'was able to travel up and down the country, arrayed as a major general in transport provided by the British military forces, and to deal, apparently on equal terms, with the highest British Commanders'.[41] When Mountbatten attempted to crack down on Aung San, it was too late.

The question of whether Mountbatten's strategy was correct is a very hard one to resolve, dependent as it is upon counterfactuals and the benefit of hindsight. That Aung San was victorious in the subsequent elections may be taken, as it was by Mountbatten himself, as a triumphant vindication of his decision to recognise him. To others, such as F.S.V.Donnison, however, the AFPFL won largely because it had successfully intimidated much of the electorate and the Burmese government servants. A 'totalitarian government', he wrote, '[had] advanced to power behind the cover of democratic institutions'.[42] Similarly, supporters of Mountbatten have laid much stress upon the fact that he enjoyed a co-operative relationship with Aung San. But to critics, this is scarcely surprising

if Aung San owed part of his influence to Mountbatten's
sponsorship. Mountbatten certainly fulfilled his promise not to hand
over to Dorman-Smith a country in chaos. But he did hand over one
with a vastly strengthened nationalist movement.

II

'You know my views on the future of Burma from the many talks
we have had', Mountbatten told Auchinleck at the end of the
Japanese war, 'and I can assure you that I have equally progressive
views about the future of Malaya, which I intend to follow as long
as I am in command in the Far East.'[43] Mountbatten had begun
planning for the future of Malaya in February 1944, when he wrote
to Ralph Hone, charged by the War Office with planning the
military   administration   of   Malaya   after   re-occupation.
Mountbatten's desire was to take advantage of the golden
opportunity that re-occupation afforded to put British rule in Malaya
'on a firmer and more rational footing'. He favoured the
strengthening of British control through the creation of a Malayan
Union. During the period of the military administration, an advisory
council should be elected by the 'more educated classes', which
might then form the basis for a legislative council under a civil
government. The hereditary sultans should not be reinstated, since
most had been active collaborators with the Japanese, but would
instead form an unelected upper house of the advisory council. This
'rationalisation', or 'tidying-up', which Mountbatten regarded as
'progressive in the sound sense of the word', should be easy to
accomplish, since it could only be opposed on 'feudal or romantic
grounds'. It might provide the basis for an enthusiastic publicity
campaign to persuade Malayans of the benefits of British rule. That
the Malay had failed to rally behind the British during the Japanese
invasion of 1942 was, Mountbatten believed, due to 'our not having
sufficiently interested ourselves in securing his co-operation'.
Instead, Mountbatten favoured what he described as 'a new attitude
... of "paternalism"', by which the Malay would be 'made to feel

that he can no longer justly accuse us of a purely mercenary neglect and indifference towards him'.[44]

In fact, Mountbatten's suggestions had already been pre-empted by work in the Colonial Office, whose Eastern Department had already drawn up a scheme for a Malayan Union, by which the power of the sultans was to be broken through the renegotiation of treaties.[45] To the complexities of their work Mountbatten was, it must be admitted, a singularly ill-informed newcomer. His proposals revealed, as Colonial Secretary Oliver Stanley pointed out as tactfully as he could, huge misconceptions about the Malayan problem. In the first place, they completely ignored the fact that Malaya was a plural society, in which no common sense of nationality had evolved, and in which communal tension between the Malay, Chinese and Indian communities was the most important factor in constitutional progress. To call immediate elections on re-occupation would be to confront the tricky decision about how far to extend the franchise to the immigrant communities. The sultans, whose position Mountbatten had airily assumed could be changed simply by 'omitting to restore what was neither necessary nor beneficial in a previous set-up', in fact enjoyed treaty rights which must be renegotiated before constitutional reform could occur. The only alternative to renegotiation was annexation. Mountbatten's desire to avoid re-instatement would involve the worst of both worlds: it would involve the breach of treaty rights, thereby antagonising the sultans, and it would then give the sultans back constitutional authority in the advisory assembly. Even the publicity campaign had its dangers, for it would allow the Japanese to play off one group against another and weaken their desire for British return.[46]

Mountbatten kept the exchange of letters going until October, though by the end it meant little. He admitted that his call for elections might have been 'premature'. Where previously he had dismissed fears that displacing the sultans would be unpopular on the grounds that they were merely autocratic and irresponsible, he now worried that the sultans were being asked to sign or resign under pressure of Britain's overwhelming force. This might be unpopular. In fact, as Stanley pointed out, how unpopular it would be would depend on whether the sultans had shown themselves to be defenders of the people under occupation, and whether they had defended the Malays, or the Chinese and Indians too. Mountbatten was also worried about the privileges being granted to the Malays, which he thought would antagonise communal relations. This was another misunderstanding. In fact, as Stanley pointed out, it was the possibility that the Malays would lose their privileges that constituted the greatest objection to the scheme.[47]

Perhaps the most extraordinary of Mountbatten's misunderstandings concerned his request, in May 1945, for permission to re-arm the Malayan Anti-Japanese Resistance Movement (AJUF) and give it the task of keeping order in the country districts where there were no Japanese. 'We have not previously found colonial subjects rising to fight on our behalf when we were about to occupy their territory', Mountbatten excitedly told his superiors. This was a perfect opportunity to demonstrate to anti-colonial critics in the US and elsewhere Britain's liberal intentions in her colonies. Mountbatten was well aware that this involved risks. 'If we back them to any appreciable extent', he warned Oliver Stanley, 'we shall owe them a special debt and give them a strong case if they choose to ask for special privileges.'[48] In fact, the risks were greater than he realised. Far from rising to fight on behalf of the British, the AJUF was dominated by Chinese Communist guerrillas dedicated to the overthrow not merely of Japanese, but of all foreign influence. It later formed the basis of the Malayan Communist Party's force, which the British dedicated twelve years to repressing. In the event, the re-occupation of Malaya was a comparatively smooth process, and Mountbatten's attempts to influence policy towards nationalist movements relatively insignificant. That its eventual decolonisation worked in British economic and strategic interests, however, owed almost everything to the ability of Mountbattten's successors to build a working alliance with the Malay community based on putting down the Communist forces Mountbatten had been keen to arm.

III

What picture of Mountbatten's ideas on the question of decolonisation does this survey give us? Whatever Mountbatten's own feelings in the matter, there were of course good operational reasons for treading carefully with liberation movements in Asia. Yet equally clearly, Mountbatten took an instinctive, if sometimes ill-informed, stance on the handling of liberation movements which differed from those of colonial administrators and his military colleagues in its willingness to dispense with Britain's traditional allies and to identify and back those who he thought to be the active elements in the emerging polities. His preference was for political concessions to mollify the activist and paternalistic socio-economic policies to win the support of the people. He was also much more aware than many of his contemporaries of the constraints on British freedom of action. In particular, he was well aware of the necessity for presenting British actions in a favourable light, especially to progressive-minded audiences at home and among Britain's wartime allies.

This peculiar and unconventional stance seems in need of explanation. Mountbatten was a generation younger than many of his fellow officers and, as such, had grown up in a climate characterised more by war and decline rather than imperial greatness. As a member of an aristocratic class now forced to come to terms with mass democracy, Mountbatten was well aware from his own experiences of the necessity for old regimes to adjust in order to survive. His treatment of the Malay sultans, as later the Indian princes, owed a good deal to his belief that aristocracies had to justify themselves through public service and the surrender of some, if not all, of their traditional privileges.[49] Perhaps, too, some of his admiration for young nationalist leaders such as Aung San sprang from identification with youthful impetuosity. Mountbatten had a lifelong preference for the active and dynamic and part of his contempt for the Burmese old guard was their unwillingness, in marked contrast to his own practice, of raising their heads above the parapet.

Undoubtedly Mountbatten's proximity to South-East Asia, so much greater than that of Dorman-Smith governing Burma from his hilltop in Simla or the Colonial Office planning the future of Malaya from Whitehall, gave him a much clearer knowledge of the far-reaching changes that the war had wrought there. However, what it did not give him, it seems, is a clear understanding of that nationalism. On his first visit to India with the Prince of Wales in 1922 he had shown considerably more interest in polo and princes than in the emergence of the nationalist movement there.[50] He tended to regard all nationalist movements as united peoples struggling to be free and was blind to the subtle conflicts of interest and ideology which divided them. The problem with this was that it was precisely upon these divisions that the ability of the British to influence the process of decolonisation rested. By exploiting the apprehension of those anxious not to be left behind in the struggle for succession, such as traditional elites fearful that their property and position would be swept away in social disorder, or regional leaders afraid that independence would mean the seizure and entrenchment of power by a single tribe, community or religious group, and by adjusting the details of constitutional plans, especially the conditions of the franchise and representation, to favour those prepared to accept progress on British terms, colonial officials could often frustrate the attempts of their opponents to weld the disparate classes of colonial societies into an effective anti-colonial alliance. In neglecting these subtleties, Mountbatten deprived himself of what had hitherto been the most powerful weapon in the colonial armoury. Thus where Mountbatten insisted that only Aung San represented the Burmese people, his protégé, Hubert Rance, a more astute observer, noted that it contained not 'true-blue Burmese patriots but [also] self-seekers into whose hands we would be playing'. British strategy should be dedicated to breaking it up into its constituent components, not building it up.[51] Mountbatten tended to present problems to his superiors in quite stark terms. In his cables to the Chiefs of Staff, he would often set out two or three possible courses of action: repression or negotiations; suppression or co-operation.[52] The Hobson's choice was, of course, to be offered most starkly by Mountbatten as Viceroy of India. Possibly this strategy was simply a means of persuasion, put forward in the hope that retreat from the unacceptable would force his superiors to accept the inevitable. Perhaps, too, it also reflects a style of thinking which is not uncommon among military officers: the desire for clear and unambiguous orders. It is not altogether clear that this was the most desirable way to approach the problems of post-war anti-colonial nationalism.

IV

When we turn our attention to Mountbatten's activities in the reoccupation of the Netherlands East Indies (NEI) and French Indo-China, a further dimension to the question appears. Mountbatten's directive instructed him to re-occupy no more of French Indo-China and the NEI than was necessary to disarm the Japanese, repatriate Allied prisoners and preserve law and order until power was duly transferred to their former colonial masters. But in each case, the local commanders found themselves dragged into conflicts between European settlers and nationalists. In Indo-China, Mountbatten's local commander, Douglas Gracey, caught between the newly declared government of Vietnam under Ho Chi Minh and the returning French, felt that he had little choice but to break the hold of the Viet Minh over Saigon in backing the French coup of 23 September. When the French troops took reprisals against the Vietnamese population aimed at consolidating their gains, the Viet

Minh responded with sabotage and road blockades. Mountbatten was anxious to limit the British commitments in the area, for 'the stronger we are the more the French will feel they can take provocative action'.[53] But keen 'to maintain a proper standard of British prestige in the eyes of the French and Chinese',[54] Gracey energetically pursued a policy of tying himself to the French re-occupation and — in a touch that would have been quite uncharacteristic of Mountbatten — refusing to talk to the Viet Minh.

Deprived of political advice and left to form his own impressions, Gracey was instinctively unsympathetic to Asian nationalism. His military career had consisted of a series of encounters in colonial theatres and he was described by a colleague as 'a Conservative of the old school ... slower to share the views of us younger men who were impatient to see independence for India and other colonial territories'.[55] He regarded the provisional government as a 'puppet government, vociferous on paper as regards democratic and even communistic plans for the future', but 'quite incapable of keeping law and order'; and its army as a rabble of armed 'hooligans' and 'criminals of the worst type'.[56] His brigadier regarded the Viet Minh as '[g]ood talkers, quite attractive men from an intellectual point of view; but of those I met, I would not have thought that executive control was ever going to be their strong suit'.[57] However, Gracey was not wholly blind to the necessity for political action. The situation, he noted, was 'an almost exact parallel with Burma. If only the French would promise progressive sovereignty and the Annamites would be equally ready to meet them, the situation might clear up.'[58] But he did not see politics as his business. Forced by Mountbatten to meet the Viet Minh government, he confined himself to lofty talk: the Viet Minh could co-operate or face Gracey's firepower 'with tanks, guns and the finest infantry in the world'.[59] Even though he deplored their excesses, he refused to put pressure on the French to make concessions to the Viet Minh. He demanded powers to use military courts and summary death sentences to break logjams in the overworked French courts, a departure that Mountbatten had ruled out in Burma.[60] This he regarded as 'not get[ting] involved politically'.[61]

But though it has been the subject of much speculation, Gracey's attitude towards colonial nationalism made little difference. Even when talks were successfully started under his auspices, between the French and Viet Minh, both sides had their hands tied: the French officials by Paris' refusal to go beyond its own modest proposals and the Viet Minh by the suspicion of its radical supporters that it might trade the principle of sovereignty. Even though Mountbatten wished Gracey would show greater enthusiasm for the negotiations, he recognised that the Foreign Office, anxious not to antagonise the French, would not accept direct pressures, and he confined his criticisms to tactical details.[62] In the absence of concessions from the French there was precious little scope for British officers to adopt a liberal policy.

As in Indo-China, SEAC troops arrived in Java some weeks after the Japanese surrender to find a functioning nationalist government, led in this case by Soekarno and Hatta, entrenched in its major towns and cities and backed by large, well-armed, if poorly trained, military forces determined to resist the return of their former colonial rulers. The British Government was keen not to offend the Dutch, but equally determined that British troops should not be deployed for any purpose other than the repatriation of prisoners, the disarmament of the Japanese and the maintenance of law and order until the return of Dutch civil administration. However, the local commander, Philip Christison, who had been warned by Browning and Mountbatten himself that he, rather than the Supreme Commander, would be expected to 'carry the can'[63] in the event of difficulties, found his troops drawn into the conflict between Dutch settlers and the Republican provisional government, and, after the death of a British brigadier attempting to calm a disturbance, into street-battles with the revolutionary youth movement for control of Surabaya. Mountbatten and Christison did their best to persuade the settlers to negotiate with the nationalists and to keep Dutch troops out of trouble, to the extent of removing their military commander, Admiral C.Helfrich, on the grounds that he turned a blind eye to their use of reprisals. All this was in marked contrast to the dilatory behaviour of Gracey in Indo-China. But the political negotiations were painfully slow, and even when a more moderate nationalist leadership emerged, anxious to treat with the Dutch, it proved unable to progress faster than its activists were prepared to allow. Once Mountbatten was satisfied that SEAC's primary tasks had been completed, he successfully advocated an early departure of British troops.

Mountbatten found it 'heartbreaking' to have to leave the political negotiations in Indo-China and NEI to the French and Dutch. 'I can assure you', he wrote to Tom Driberg, 'that if I was left as free a hand in French Indo-China and the Netherlands East Indies as I was left in Burma, I could solve both these problems by the same methods.'[64] But though Mountbatten frequently lectured his French and Dutch colleagues on the need to deal with Asian nationalists, basing his arguments on the success he believed he had achieved with Aung San in Burma,[65] the analogy was far from perfect.

In the first place, the French and Dutch were in a much weaker military position than the British had been in Burma and Malaya. Where the British found it possible to step back into their old colonies rapidly after the Japanese defeat, there was a crucial gap between the defeat of the Japanese and the arrival of SEAC troops in the former Dutch and French colonies. By the time the British took control of Rangoon, the Japanese were in headlong retreat. But in the cases of Indo-China and the NEI, they had remained in place, encouraging the nationalist movements against the return of European colonial powers. Where the British had fought their way across Burma and enjoyed an extensive military presence there, which gave them the ability to negotiate with the nationalists from a relative position of strength, the French possessed only small, under-equipped and ill-trained forces in the SEAC theatre, despite their best efforts to persuade their allies to permit re-inforcements to be shipped east, while the Dutch were almost wholly reliant upon the United States for training and equipment. Indeed, returning on the coat-tails of the British, they felt all the more acutely the necessity to restore their military prestige. Worse still, both the French and the Dutch leaders also suffered badly from the absence of effective political intelligence. The French military commander, General Philippe Leclerc, and High Commissioner Thierry D'Argenlieu were stuck in Kandy and Chandernagor near Calcutta until the start and end of October respectively, reliant upon patchy intelligence reports for news. The Dutch intelligence services were small, thinly equipped and hampered by friction with SOE and the hostility of the local population and consistently underestimated the strength of the Republican forces.[66]

Secondly, in the period of anarchy between Japanese defeat and the arrival of SEAC, nationalist groups had gained a much greater ascendancy in French Indo-China and the Netherlands East Indies than they had managed in Malaya or Burma. By the time the French arrived in any numbers in Indo-China, Ho Chi Minh had not merely declared the Democratic Republic of Vietnam, but had moved to take over the administration of several major cities in northern Tonkin. The Dutch too found themselves facing not, as had Mountbatten in Burma, lightly armed dacoits, but an established republican army of resistance. The returning forces were therefore faced with a much harder task of displacement than Mountbatten had faced in the British colonies.

Thirdly, the nationalist groups with which the French and Dutch military were confronted seemed less *politically* acceptable than had their counterparts to the British in Burma, Malaya and

Ceylon. While the Japanese remained undefeated, Mountbatten could argue to his political superiors that operational necessity dictated unpalatable concessions. Parallel arguments could not be made by the Dutch or French commanders. Soekarno had collaborated with, not fought against, the Japanese, who had in any case surrendered by the time SEAC arrived in Java, so there was no military reason to enlist his support. It was therefore impossible for Dutch commanders to argue, as had Mountbatten to his political superiors over Aung San, that he had 'worked his passage home' and was therefore entitled to political concessions. In the case of Indo-China, there were other complications. Not only was Ho Chi Minh a former Comintern agent, a fact which caused great anxiety in France, but his soldiers possessed a much more radical leftist programme than Aung San. This made repression more likely, partly because recognition of a Communist succession in Indo-China was considered politically unacceptable by the French government, anxious not to give succour to political opponents at home, and also increasingly to the United States, which might otherwise have acted as a restraining influence on French excesses.

The French and Dutch commanders thus lacked the necessary mandate from their political masters to negotiate with nationalist groups. Wartime planning for the colonies had been much harder for the displaced European governments-in-exile than it had been for the British Colonial Office. Moreover, even the plans that had been made were heavily contested within the new governments established after the liberation of Europe. This marked a further contrast with the British position. In Ceylon, constitutional progress had been set firmly on a course to independence when, in 1938, cabinet government had been put in place.[67] The familiar promise that Burma would enjoy no less privileged treatment than India and the new intentions stated in the White Paper of May 1945 gave Mountbatten a clear and helpful political direction to follow. In Malaya, as we have seen, the War Cabinet had a plan of advance in readiness which, though unannounced until January 1946, had been privately known to Mountbatten since May 1944. The arrival in office of Attlee's Labour government, with its tradition of sympathy for colonial freedom, made the destination of British policy even clearer. In the French and Dutch cases, however, there was little tradition of constitutional progress on which to build. In the case of France, though the Brazzaville Conference had made it clear that devolution of power was possible, even within an indivisible republic, it had insisted that freedom be defined in terms of acceptance of French citizenship. Moreover, the reconciliation of metropolitan and colonial interests that it represented depended, as Martin Shipway has suggested, upon a shaky domestic consensus: in particular, deep ideological fractures in the party system, reflected in a divided legislature, unstable coalition government and the bifurcation of political authority between Paris and Colombey-les-Deux-Églises.[68] Under such circumstances, the *politique de Brazzaville* could not readily be sustained. Deprived of clear instructions from the politicians of the left at home, French commanders, especially those ex-*Maquisards* who had been appointed by De Gaulle, preferred to wait on their leader's return rather than chance an open-ended negotiation with Ho Chi Minh. Indeed, it was part of the political culture of the French Army, reinforced by the events of 1940, that national honour could, under certain circumstances, justify ignoring, or even disobedience to the politicians in Paris. Although in December 1942 the Dutch government-in-exile had offered a post-war conference to discuss the devolution of power over internal affairs to the constituent parts of the empire, its proposals lacked both detail and conviction. The 'liberation' coalition government contained a strongly conservative Catholic party dedicated to the liquidation of the Indonesian Republic.[69] Whatever Mountbatten's liberal instincts, they owed much of their influence to the fact that they were in tune with the policy of his political masters. There was much less scope for French and Dutch commanders to push policy in a different direction.

Partly, doubtless this was simply due to the fact that, put crudely, the recovery of colonial territory was regarded as essential to the restoration of national pride and integrity and as a means of winning popular support in political wrangles at home. Partly too, it was because while South-East Asia lay on the fringes of the British imperial system, centred on India, for France and the Netherlands, it lay at the heart of their presence in the east. The costs of losing territory there were thought to be considerable, especially by the Dutch, who remained (quite wrongly, as it turned out) convinced that retention of the Indies was vital to the post-war recovery of their extensively damaged economy. Moreover, in the Netherlands, as in France, the question of the treatment of Asian nationalists was inextricably bound up with the treatment of collaborators at home. The newly-installed 'liberation' governments in Paris and the Hague could not easily countenance negotiations with anti-colonial collaborators in the east at the same time as they prosecuted those who had collaborated at home, particularly if those negotiations were at the expense of loyalists who had fought to protect Dutch interests and suffered years of imprisonment at the hands of the Japanese. Here again there was no British parallel.

A final, and perhaps key, variable in the re-occupation was the position of expatriate settlers. In Java, there was a substantial population of recently released exiles and expatriates, whose fears that SEAC would not help them drove them to band together for strength, itself regarded as a provocation by the Republicans. In his resignation letter to Mountbatten, Helfrich pointed out that the aggressive methods of his troops against Indonesian civilians and Republican politicians, though regrettable, were only to be expected given the fact that 2,000 women and children, most of them the families of military personnel, were starving in internment camps run by Soekarno's Republican guards, while SEAC refused to allow Dutch reinforcements to land.[70] In French Indo-China, there was a similar population in Saigon. Many of them had only been displaced the previous March when the Japanese removed the Vichy administration and installed in its place a puppet Vietnamese government under the Emperor of Annam, Bao Dai. In the anarchic days after the collapse of the Japanese, the settler community had been subject to attack and harassment and looked to the French forces to re-establish their position. It was at the instigation of these settlers and with the enthusiastic assistance of their small army (the Eleventh Régiment d'Infanterie Coloniale) that the Viet Minh government was ejected from its Saigon strongholds in the coup of 23 September. French commanders on the spot were well aware that the settler population constituted a liability. 'They do not understand the situation', commented Jean Cédile, 'and are unaware that the present state of international relations has created obligations more than rights. They think they have only rights.'[71] But in the absence of other troops he was forced to use them, and to dismiss as unacceptable to Paris the suggestion of Mountbatten's political adviser, H.N.Brain, that they should be evacuated. Where Mountbatten could order that no Burmese collaborator should be punished for beliefs sincerely held, French settlers in Saigon forced Cedile to threaten treason charges against those who had collaborated with the Japanese.[72] All in all, the British military, never so deeply engaged in the practice of colonial rule and without the complication of fellow countrymen and women in danger, were less likely to identify with settler groups or with the preservation of a specifically colonial form of international influence.

V

Much of the case for Mountbatten's liberalism rests upon contrasts between his actions and beliefs and those of his French and Dutch counterparts. Certainly the French and Dutch forces contained their share of die-hards, such as Lieutenant Colonel Jacques Massu, who firmly believed that the resistance of the Viet Minh was 'merely a surface phenomenon', and Helfrich, who held that 'when dealing with native rabbles the most profitable way was to hit immediately and hit hard.'[73] D'Argenlieu, the French High Commissioner to

whom the military officers were subordinate and who jealously
guarded his responsibility for political progress, was also a
cloistered mind, perhaps traceable to the fact that his naval career
had been preceded by twenty years as a Carmelite monk. But they
also had liberal-minded soldiers. Leclerc, despite the tactics that he
employed in Indo-China, cannot be regarded simply as a die-hard.
'One does not kill ideas with bullets', he once observed in a fashion
similar to that of Mountbatten.[74] 'Traitez, traitez, à tout prix', he
told the new High Commissioner after D'Argenlieu.[75] Brain
regarded Cédile as 'a well meaning and liberal-minded man';[76]
Van Mook, the Dutch Minister for the Colonies, was also regarded
in British circles as a liberal.[77]

In Mountbatten's shoes, these men might well have
followed a similar line. But the constraints that they faced made it
all but impossible for a liberal policy to be employed. 'What you
say makes sense', Leclerc told Slim and Mountbatten when urged
to model his policy on the British strategy in Burma, 'but is not
French policy.'[78] When he passed on the British suggestion to De
Gaulle, proposing that some form of dominion status be introduced
in Indo-China, he was given a flat rejection: retreat in the face of
threats, especially at British prompting, was politically unacceptable
at home.[79] The most they could do was to attempt to ensure that
while military force was employed to acquire greater leverage at the
negotiating table and thereby break the hold of the nationalists over
the process of decolonisation, it was accompanied by political
concessions.

Mountbatten's ability to countenance political concessions
to South-East Asian nationalists thus rested to a large degree upon
the fact that he enjoyed advantages that were denied to Leclerc and
Van Mook. In particular, he possessed reliable troops unaffected by
ties of loyalty to expatriate settlers and clear political instructions,
at least insofar as they concerned British interests. To see how
significant these advantages were, we have only to imagine how

much harder it would have been for Mountbatten to follow his chosen course had he been forced to rely upon an army of disaffected Burmese planters, or had he arrived in Malaya to find the Malayan Communist Party ensconced in power. Helfrich once tellingly compared Soekarno and Hatta with the former Indian National Congress leader, Subhas Chandra Bose, whose Indian National Army (INA) had fought with the Japanese during the war and who, unlike Aung San, had failed to switch sides. Mountbatten dismissed the comparison as 'having no bearing on the matter', but in fact it was a revealing one.[80] The British deeply resented the activities of the INA, especially where they had attacked loyalists, and after the war attempted to try several of its officers for war crimes. Had Mountbatten been forced to rely on the INA for support, he would have found it much harder to persuade politicians at home of the necessity for concessions.

The trajectories of the European decolonisations in Asia were greatly divergent, ranging from smooth and orderly transfers of power to intense racial wars. The contributions of European military forces were correspondingly varied. While acknowledging that the perceptions and prejudices of military leaders played a significant part in determining their course, and that it is therefore important to characterise them accurately, it has been argued here that — however enlightened — they were but a single factor in more complex equations.

References

This paper is based on a presentation given at 'Mountbatten on the Record', a conference held at Southampton University in April 1996. I am very grateful to the organisers and participants for their advice and many helpful comments. I also owe a great deal to Dr Chris Woolgar and his colleagues at the Hartley Institute for helping me to find materials in the Mountbatten Archive during my time as a Visiting Fellow.

1   *Emergencies and disorder in the European empires after 1945* ed. R.F.Holland (London, 1994); F.Furedi *Colonial wars and the politics of Third World nationalism* (London, 1994); S.L.Carruthers *Winning hearts and minds: British governments, the media and colonial counter-insurgency, 1944-60* (Leicester, 1995).

2   Quoted in P.Ziegler *Mountbatten: the official biography* (London, 1985) p. 692.

3   A.Roberts *Eminent Churchillians* (London, 1994).

4   *BSI* i, pp. 42-4: note by Sir Reginald Dorman-Smith, 22 Sep 1944; USL MB1/C249, Dorman-Smith to Mountbatten, 10 Mar 1944.

5   USL MB1/C249, Mountbatten to Dorman-Smith, 1 Aug 1944.

6   PRO CAB 66/WP(44)299, Mountbatten to Chiefs of Staff, 22 May 1944, printed as annexe to Ceylon Constitution, 7 Jun 1944.

7   USL MB1/C252, Mountbatten to Stanley, 6 Sep 1944.

8   *BSI* i, pp. 60-1, 207-8: Advanced HQ, SACSEA to Rear HQ, 11th Army Group, 18 Apr 1944; HQ, Supreme Allied Commander, South East Asia, SAC (Misc.) 6th Meeting, 2 Apr 1945.

9   M.R.D.Foot *SOE: an outline history of the Special Operations Executive, 1940-46* (London, 1984) p. 214. See also Charles Cruickshank *SOE in the Far East* (Oxford, 1983).

10   *BSI* i, pp. 470-2: Rance to Mountbatten, 14 Sep 1945.

11   *BSI* i, pp. 490-1: Stopford to Mountbatten, 26 Sep 1945.

12   *BSI* i, pp. 153-4, 163-6, 171: Mackenzie to Mountbatten, 31 Jan 1945; Prescott to Advanced HQ, ALFSEA, 13 Feb 1945; Operations Branch to Chief of Staff ALFSEA, 13 Feb 1945; Mountbatten to Leese, 27 Feb 1945. IOLR MSS Eur E 362/4, F.S.V.Donnison, 'Memoir'.

13   *BSI* i, pp. 205-6: Wise to Dorman-Smith, 30 Mar 1945.

14   *BSI* i, pp. 163-5: Prescott to Advanced HQ, ALFSEA, 13 Feb 1945.

15   *BSI* i, pp. 153-4: Mackenzie to Mountbatten, 31 Jan 1945.

16   *BSI* i, p. 238: Advanced HQ, ALFSEA to Mountbatten, 9 May 1945; Mountbatten to Advanced HQ, ALFSEA, 9 May 1945.

17   *BSI* i, pp. 260-1, 264-5, 273-5, 284-5: Mountbatten to Chiefs of Staff, 16

May 1945; Dorman-Smith to Mountbatten, 18 May 1945; Chiefs of Staff to Mountbatten, 22 May 1945; Dorman-Smith to Pearce, 25 May 1945.

18   *BSI* i, pp. 335-7: record of Mountbatten's meeting with Civil Affairs Officers, 16 Jun 1945.

19   *Personal diary of Admiral the Lord Louis Mountbatten, Supreme Allied Commander, South-East Asia, 1943-1946* ed. P.Ziegler (London, 1988) p. 206, entries for 8-15 May.

20   *BSI* i, pp. 320-3: Mountbatten to Browning, 12 Jun 1945.

21   IOLR MSS Eur E 362/18, Wise, 'Memoir'.

22   *BSI* i, pp. 197-9: Mountbatten to Chiefs of Staff, 27 Mar 1945.

23   PRO CAB 91/3, War Cabinet, India Committee Meeting I(45)15(2), 29 Mar 1945.

24   *BSI* i, pp. 153-4: Mackenzie to Mountbatten, 31 Jan 1945.

25   *BSI* i, pp. 205-6: Wise to Dorman-Smith, 30 Mar 1945.

26   Such a technique was favoured by British PM, Winston Churchill. See *BSI* i, pp. 87-8, 117: Amery to Dorman-Smith, 11 Oct 1944; Churchill to Stuart, 3 Dec 1944.

27   Quoted in P.Dennis *Troubled days of peace: Mountbatten and South East Asia Command, 1945-46* (Manchester, 1987) pp. 11-12.

28   *BSI* i, pp. 214-15: Joubert to Mountbatten, 7 Apr 1945.

29   USL MB1/C249, Mountbatten, 'Note on Burma', 2 Oct 1944.

30   PRO WO 203/4327, Auchinleck to Mountbatten, 24 Aug 1945.

31   *BSI* i, pp. 207-8: HQ, Supreme Allied Commander, South East Asia, SAC (Misc.) 6th Meeting, 2 Apr 1945.

32   *BSI* i, pp. 205-6: Wise to Dorman-Smith, 30 Mar 1945.

33   *BSI* i, pp. 163-5: Prescott to Advanced HQ, ALFSEA, 13 Feb 1945; PRO CAB 91/3, War Cabinet, India Committee Meeting I(45)15(2), 29 Mar 1945.

34   *BSI* i, pp. 209-14: HQ, Supreme Allied Commander, South East Asia SAC (Misc.) 7th Meeting, 5 Apr 1945.

35   For a detailed consideration of the policy, N.Tarling, 'Lord Mountbatten and the return of civil government to Burma' *Journal of Imperial and Commonwealth History* 11 (1983) pp. 197-226.

36   *BSI* i, pp. 408-10: Weekly Intelligence Summary, 25 Aug 1945.

37   IOLR MSS Eur E 362/4, Donnison, 'Memoir'.

38   *BSI* i, pp. 366-7, 372-6: Wallace to Rance, 13 July 1945; HQ Meeting, 15 July 1945.

39   *BSI* i, pp. 244-6, 480-4: Lindop to Rance, 11 May 1945; MacDougall, 'Note on Background of Kandy Conference', 20 Sep 1945.

40   *BSI* i, pp. 384-6: Dorman-Smith to Amery, 25 Jul 1945.

41   IOLR MSS Eur E 362/18, Wise, 'Memoir'.

42   IOLR MSS Eur E 362/4, Donnison, 'Memoir'.

43   PRO WO 203/4327, Mountbatten to Auchinleck, 30 Aug 1945.

44   USL MB1/C123/3, Mountbatten to Hone, 4 Feb 1944; MB1/C252, Mountbatten to Cranborne, 19 Mar 1944.

45   See *Malaya* ed. A.J.Stockwell (British Documents on the End of Empire, Series B, 1-3; 1995) i, pp. 64-70: Future Constitutional Policy for British Colonial Territories in South-East Asia, 14 Jan 1944.

46   USL MB1/C252, Stanley to Mountbatten, 13 Jun 1944.

47   MB1/C252, Mountbatten to Stanley, 29 Jul 1944; Stanley to Mountbatten, 21 Aug 1944; Mountbatten to Stanley, 6 Sep 1944; Stanley to Mountbatten, 17 Oct 1944.

48   MB1/C252, Mountbatten to Stanley, 11 May 1945.

49   See D.Cannadine *The decline and fall of the British aristocracy* (New Haven and London, 1990) pp. 606-36.

50   Ziegler, *Mountbatten*, pp. 60-3.

51   *BSI* i, pp. 278-9: Rance to Joubert, 22 May 1945.

52   For examples, Dennis, *Troubled days of peace*, pp. 105-6, 148-50.

53   PRO WO 203/4020, Mountbatten to War Office, 24 Sep 1945.

54   Quoted in Dennis, *Troubled days of peace*, p. 173.

55   P.M.Dunn *The first Vietnam War* (London, 1985) p. 163. Gracey had been born in India and was commissioned in the Indian Army in 1914. He later held appointments in the Middle East (Palestine and Persia) and India, and commanded the 20th Indian Division.

56   Quoted in Dunn, *First Vietnam War*, pp. 164-5.

57   Dunn, *First Vietnam War*, pp. 171-2.

58   Dunn, *First Vietnam War*, p. 187.

59   Quoted in Dennis, *Troubled days of peace*, p. 63.

60   Dennis, *Troubled days of peace*, p. 168.

61   Dunn, *First Vietnam War*, p. 209.

62   Dennis, *Troubled days of peace*, p. 167.

63   Dennis, *Troubled days of peace*, p. 87.

64   USL MB1/C91, Mountbatten to Driberg, undated.

65   Examples are quoted in Dennis, *Troubled days of peace*, p. 95.

66   Bob de Graaff, 'Hot intelligence in the tropics: Dutch intelligence operations in the Netherlands East Indies during the Second World War' *Journal of Contemporary History* 22 (1987) pp. 563-84; Dennis, *Troubled days of peace*, pp. 74-8.

67   K.M. De Silva *A history of Sri Lanka* (Berkeley, CA, 1981) p. 461.

68   Martin Shipway, 'Creating an emergency: metropolitan constraints on French colonial policy and its breakdown in Indo-China, 1945-47' in *Emergencies and disorder*, pp. 1-16.

69   P.M.H.Groen, 'Militant response: the Dutch use of military force and the decolonization of the Dutch East Indies, 1945-50' in *Emergencies and*

disorder, pp. 30-44.

70   USL MB1/C123, Helfrich to Mountbatten, 24 Jan 1946.
71   Quoted in Dennis, *Troubled days of peace*, pp. 61-2.
72   Dennis, *Troubled days of peace*, pp. 95, 164.
73   Dennis, *Troubled days of peace*, pp. 153, 173.
74   Quoted in Anthony Clayton *Three Marshals of France: leadership after trauma* (London, 1992) p. 127.
75   Clayton, *Three Marshals*, p. 136.
76   Dennis, Troubled days of peace, p. 62.
77   *Malaya*, i, pp. 8-9: Minutes of Meeting with Dr Van Mook, 12 Jun 1942.
78   Clayton, *Three Marshals*, p. 127.
79   Dennis, *Troubled days of peace*, pp. 52, 65.
80   PRO CAB 105/162, Mountbatten to Chiefs of Staff, 1 Oct 1945.

CHAPTER 3

The Mountbatten Viceroyalty Revisited: Themes and Controversies

Ian Talbot
Coventry University

The literature on the transfer of power in India is extensive and highly polemical. None more so than on the role of Lord Mountbatten. His numerous admirers depict him as indispensable in resolving the constitutional deadlock which threatened civil war in India. This paved the way for a swift British departure which crucially was on good terms with their erstwhile nationalist opponents. His critics however see him as being responsible for the Punjab massacres that accompanied the Partition and maintain that his bias towards the Congress contributed to subsequent Indo-Pakistan hostility. This has come to be symbolised by, if not encapsulated by, the Kashmir dispute and continues to exert a doleful impact on Indo-Pakistan relations nearly half a century later.

The debates on Lord Mountbatten's role are vigorous and historiographically significant. Those who have largely lauded his endeavours as Viceroy include his official biographer, Philip Ziegler;[1] colleagues such as Lord Ismay,[2] H.V.Hodson,[3] W.H.Morris-Jones[4] and, of course, Alan Campbell-Johnson;[5] professional historians such as Robin Moore;[6] and the more journalistically inclined Collins and Lapierre in *Freedom at midnight*.[7] Subcontinental critics include the Pakistani writers, Chaudhri Muhammad Ali,[8] M.A.H.Ispahani[9] and Latif Ahmed Sherwani;[10] and such Indian historians as Y.Krishan[11] and Bipin Chandra.[12] Their chorus has been swelled from Britain by Leonard Mosley,[13] Alastair Lamb[14] and, more recently, Andrew Roberts,[15] who has reopened the debate about Lord Mountbatten's alleged interference with the boundary awards which accompanied Partition.

The rapidly approaching golden jubilee of the British transfer of power provides a good opportunity to take stock of this literature. The aim of this paper is not to produce a balance sheet on Lord Mountbatten's Viceroyalty. Rather it seeks to identify the main areas of contention, to trace the evolution of the historical debates and to indicate where fresh perspectives might be opened up. Before turning to the controversies, it is necessary to make some introductory remarks concerning the historical discourse on the Viceroyalty, followed by a brief description of the political situation which greeted Mountbatten when his York aircraft touched down at Palam airfield in Delhi on 22 March 1947.

I

Historical criticism of the Mountbatten Viceroyalty has tended to focus on two separate but interrelated sets of questions: first, could the massacres and mass migrations which disfigured the British departure in North-West India have been avoided by a more leisurely transfer of power? Second, was Lord Mountbatten an impartial figure in the disputes between the Congress and the Muslim League, or did he favour the former's interests in such key issues as boundary demarcation and the accession of the princely states to the two new dominions? Such controversy should by no means surprise us, as the nature of Mountbatten's task was such that it would inevitably create enemies amongst those Indian politicians who found that he could not square the circle of conflicting claims. Moreover, the parachuting in of a young, brash and somewhat radical Viceregal team invariably ruffled the feathers of more conservative members of the services who were correspondingly quick to carp and criticise. What is surprising, however, is that the debates today remain virtually unaltered from the polemics which accompanied his climacteric Viceroyalty. They also appear rather old-fashioned in their emphasis on the role of the individual single-handedly shaping great historical events.

The repetition of old issues regarding the British role in the transfer of power stands in marked contrast to the historiographical reassessment which has taken place regarding the contributions of the Congress and the Muslim League. Jinnah's intentions in raising the Pakistan demand have been the subject of a major revision following the publication of Ayesha Jalal's work, *The sole spokesman*,[16] while the studies of the Cambridge School have posited a much less powerful Indian nationalist movement than had been traditionally assumed.[17]

It is important to turn now to a contextualisation of Lord Mountbatten's Viceroyalty in order to assess the possibilities and problems which he inherited. The issue from 1942 onwards had been not whether the British should leave, but when and how quickly. However, as in many end of empire situations, the signalling of the intent to withdraw intensified political conflict amongst communities competing to control the future levers of power. Thus from the 1942 Cripps offer of dominion status onwards, 'the crisis of Indian nationhood' became increasingly interlinked with 'the crisis of empire'. The central issue was the ability of the British to impose a solution in the event of the Congress's and Muslim League's failure to agree. For again, common to many decolonisation processes, their prestige and authority as rulers diminished the nearer their departure loomed. Wavell from the beginning of 1946 onwards had realised that the key was to stay ahead of the game and control the circumstances of the British departure. Ironically, considerable power would have to be exerted in order to give it up.

The prospects were not good. The steel frame of the ICS had corroded with rust during the war years as a result of manpower shortage.[18] The morale of the largely Indianised services was further undermined by the vociferous demands for enquiries into the repression of the Quit India movement made by Nehru following his release from Almora gaol. It was not just the collapse of the administrative machinery, however, which imperilled an orderly transfer of power. It was further endangered by the constitutional deadlock between the Congress and the Muslim League at the All-India level and by growing communal and class conflict in the localities.

The Telengana uprising[19] and the Royal Indian Navy revolt[20] notwithstanding, Sumit Sarkar[21] and others have exaggerated the extent to which India stood on the brink of a socialist revolution in 1946. A communal civil war, however, posed a much greater threat to the British goal of an amicable and controlled withdrawal from the Subcontinent. While the British were able to douse the flames of nationalist or communist riot in the towns, no imperial fire brigade could deal with a communal conflagration engulfing the vast tracts of rural India. Most of the energies of the latter half of Wavell's Viceroyalty were devoted to averting this danger by brokering an All-India political settlement between the Congress and the Muslim League.

Wavell had not created this problem. It had been his predecessor, Lord Linlithgow, who had raised Jinnah's stock as leader of the All-India Muslim League in his 1940 August Offer. The creation of a counterbalance to the non-co-operating Congress had suited the war-torn Indian Empire. Thereafter Jinnah exercised a virtual veto on future constitutional advance. Simultaneously he became the symbolic focus of Muslim aspirations for self-rule.[22] His adroitness was most clearly demonstrated at the June 1945 Simla Conference, which was designed by Wavell to break the communal deadlock in the post-war era. The conference collapsed over Jinnah's demand that all members of the Indian Executive Council should belong to the Muslim League. Wavell thence had a difficult row to hoe. The Muslim League's acceptance in May 1946 of the

Cabinet Mission's three-tiered constitutional structure within a United India initially raised hopes of a political settlement. These were to be subsequently dashed on 29 July, when the Muslim League Council meeting at Bombay withdrew its agreement in the light of the Congress's attitude to the grouping scheme.

The Cabinet Mission's failure was followed by the Great Calcutta Killing of 16-18 August. Further evidence of the mounting communal crisis emerged in October when Muslim attacks on Hindus at Noakhali in East Bengal were followed by revenge killings in Bihar, which claimed, according to the Muslim League, some 40,000 lives.[23] At a conference held in the wake of the disorders, the Bengal Governor warned that his police force had degenerated into an ill-disciplined rabble and that he could not 'carry Bengal for another 12 months' because after that there would be no Bengal to carry.[24] 'Our time in India is limited', a wearied Wavell noted in his journal, 'And our power to control events almost gone. We have prestige and previous momentum to trade on and they will not last long. My task now is to secure the safest and most dignified withdrawal possible.'[25]

His solution was for a phased withdrawal. This Breakdown Plan, as it was known, had been mooted as early as 10 August. Wavell personally pressed it on the British Cabinet following the failure of a London conference of Indian political leaders on 3-6 December. He also raised for the first time the need for a termination date of the transfer of power, fixing this as no later than 31 March 1948.

Wavell's proposals were considered defeatist by the Labour Government and his candour was not well received, nor was it reciprocated. Attlee in fact broached Lord Mountbatten about taking over as Viceroy, while the December discussions with the Indian Cabinet Committee were still proceeding. The grounds for the Viceroy's dismissal were 'inconsistency'. Few would quibble with

Wavell's disillusioned comment that it was 'not very courteously done'.[26] Lord Mountbatten's appointment was simultaneously announced with the historic 20 February statement by Attlee. This declared that the British intended to leave India by June 1948.

The incoming Viceroy not only brought with him the advantages of youth, dynamism and the glamour of his royal connections, but he also benefited from the more realistic attitudes in Whitehall regarding the Indian situation. Indeed, the idea of a definite deadline for a transfer of power had been bequeathed him, as we have just noted, by Wavell although many years later Earl Mountbatten was to claim that a terminal date had been fixed at his insistence.[27] Its existence was to prove far more important for the success of his Viceroyalty than his alleged 'plenipotentiary powers'. In fact Lord Mountbatten reported extensively to the Labour Cabinet and journeyed to London in person to secure agreement to the 3 June Partition Plan.

Hindsight can underestimate the problems at the commencement of the Mountbatten Viceroyalty. While the failure of the Cabinet Mission Plan, for example, had realistically narrowed down the options for a settlement to some kind of Partition scheme, there was no reason to expect that its application would be easy. The Muslim League was to cavil at the partition of Bengal and Punjab, while Congress feared a fragmentation of the Subcontinent, hence Nehru's 'famous explosion' when he was presented on 10 May with a draft of Plan Balkan, which envisaged a transfer of power to the provinces. Moreover, the announcement of a definite deadline, rather than concentrating the mind, had sparked off bitter communal disturbances in the Punjab province.[28] The disorders were particularly serious because of the region's proximity to New Delhi, its strategic importance as the major recruiting area of the Indian Army and its volatile Muslim, Hindu and Sikh 'martial races'. The Governor, Sir Evan Jenkins, ominously reported to the Viceroy on 16 April that 'the Punjab is not now in a constitutional but in a revolutionary situation'.[29]

II

Critics and apologists both agree that the hallmark of the Mountbatten Viceroyalty was speed and decisive action. The tone was set by the brief, 15-minute, swearing-in ceremony in the Durbar Hall on 24 March. The sense of urgency after the agreement of the 3 June Partition Plan was highlighted by the printed calendars in Mountbatten's office which counted down the number of days to the British departure.

Both in his 'Report on the Last Viceroyalty' in September 1948[30] and in a speech to the East India Association in London the following month, Lord Mountbatten argued that his acceleration of the transfer of power from 30 June 1948 to 15 August 1947 had been carefully thought out. The risk of going early outweighed the disadvantages in waiting of 'continued and increasing riots'.[31] On closer examination, however, the situation is not so cut and dried. Collins and Lapierre present the announcement on 4 June as a veritable bolt from the blue.[32] Equally puzzling is the fact that Lord Mountbatten seemed to have overlooked earlier advice on the division of the armed forces when making it. On 25 April, Field Marshal Auchinleck, the Commander-in-Chief, had warned that it would be impossible to divide the Indian Army by June 1948.[33] The Viceroy apparently concurred that a hasty splitting up of the armed forces would be a 'dangerous risk'.[34]

Critics such as Mosley and Chandra have seized on this knowledge to claim that the speed of the British departure was an abdication of responsibility and a major cause of the Punjab massacres.[35] Before examining the debate on this matter, it is important to consider the motives for the acceleration of the transfer of power. Although they have been dwarfed by the controversy over its consequences, I would argue that they provide a much greater key to an understanding of the Mountbatten Viceroyalty.

Richard Hough's claims that the advancement of the date was linked with Mountbatten's wish to get back to the Navy and because the November 1947 Royal Wedding was in his mind can be almost immediately dismissed.[36] Equally implausible is the suggestion that 15 August was chosen to coincide with the second anniversary of the Japanese surrender. Andrew Roberts takes this at face value, although the formal instrument of surrender was in fact signed on 2 September 1945.[37] The Indian writer, Y.Krishan, has argued forcefully that the rationale for an early departure date was the desire to keep India in the Commonwealth. Both Alan Campbell-Johnson's diary and Philip Ziegler's biographical study reveal the significance which Britain attached to Indian membership and to Mountbatten's skilful role in securing this. As I pointed out in 1984, however, during my debate with Krishan, a major weakness in this argument is that it tells only half the story. Pressures from below also influenced Mountbatten's deliberations. Fear of being caught in the middle of a civil war which the Government of India would be powerless to control was an equally, if not even more, compelling factor in fixing the date of the transfer of power. On reflection I would add another level of argument which diminishes still further Lord Mountbatten's room for manoeuvre. What was crucial in the period April to June 1947 in determining the speed of the British departure was not only the fear of communal civil war, but the Congress response to this. A combination of cynicism regarding Pakistan's future prospects, weariness after years of opposition and a desire not to inherit a Subcontinent in flames, led its high command to press for a rapid British withdrawal. Lord Mountbatten acceded to these demands not because, as Andrew Roberts argues, he lacked toughness,[38] or grasped 'at every straw' to secure India's entry into the Commonwealth,[39] but rather because he realised that the Congress's continued co-operation was vital to an orderly British departure. Instead of supremely shaping events as Collins and

Lapierre portray, the Viceroy reacted to Indian pressures.

This important fact is overlooked by such critics as Chandra, Mosley and Roberts, who hold Lord Mountbatten personally responsible for the Punjab massacres which accompanied Partition. The first writer quotes Brigadier Bristow's view that the Punjab tragedy would not have occurred had partition been deferred for a year or so.[40] Roberts, picking up on Mosley's criticisms a generation earlier, has maintained that although in Mountbatten's judgement, speed of transfer might avoid the troubles, 'in practice his decision precipitated them. It was a situation entirely of his own making.'[41]

Roberts seeks to substantiate this bold claim by drawing attention not only to the administrative chaos created by a rapid transfer of power, but to Mountbatten's suppression of the decisions of the Punjab Boundary Award until the second day after independence. This delay, according to Roberts, was intended to ensure that the day of independence was one of triumph and not of bickering. It crucially prevented the movement of populations under 'British troops and authority' which might well have 'avoided the atmosphere of anarchy and terror which led to so much bloodshed'.[42] Once again in the great man of history genre, the plight of thousands of ordinary Muslims, Hindus and Sikhs is depicted as hanging in the balance because the Viceroy chose at this particular moment in time to 'back-pedal' on the publication of the Boundary Award.

Detailed investigations of conditions in the Punjab from March 1947 onwards reveal a steadily deteriorating law and order situation. This was rooted far more deeply than in a hasty British departure from the Subcontinent, or in the delayed publication of the Boundary Award. The violence was occasioned both by a cycle of revenge killings and by what we would now term 'ethnic cleansing'. Indeed Sikh raiding parties were launching attacks on Muslim villages in 'border' areas well before the publication of the Boundary Award.[43] In a communal war of succession which had raged from March 1947, non-Muslims were driven from Lahore[44] and Muslims from Amritsar in a sustained arson campaign.[45] The Congress and Muslim League high commands found it easier to blame 'callous' British officials for the disorders than their own local supporters who had become uncontrollable. The later charges against Lord Mountbatten form part of this wider historical pattern.

The juggernaut of communal hatred and disorder which politicians had set in motion to serve their own interests, ran out of control in August 1947 in an orgy of retaliatory killings. Despite repeated appeals by the Sikh leaders, Master Tara Singh and Giani Kartar Singh, the jathas set about their bloody business in the East Punjab. In Lahore and elsewhere in Pakistan Punjab, Muslims rounded on the remaining Hindu and Sikh inhabitants, putting paid to their leaders' smug assurance that the violence would cease when the British had departed.[46] The Punjab's tragedy involved at a most conservative estimate a quarter of a million deaths[47] and the greatest displacement of people ever, in this century of the refugee. Such an immense upheaval cannot be blamed on any single individual. Hindu, Muslim and Sikh politicians all cynically manipulated religious sentiment for their own ends. When the communal genie was out of the bottle, it was too late to attempt to recork it. Once the killings commenced, what has been termed a kind of collective madness held sway until it spent itself in exhaustion. A more balanced approach to the 1947 massacres than has been taken of late would acknowledge the importance of these impersonal forces, while at the same time recognising that, in the event, Lord Mountbatten's security arrangements were inadequate.

Robin Jeffrey,[48] for example, has demonstrated that the Viceroy gravely overestimated the ability of Major General Rees' Punjab Boundary Force to maintain law and order in a vast 37,500 square mile border area, inhabited by over 15 million people. The force was ill-equipped, comprised of a majority of emotionally involved Punjabi troops and declined rapidly in morale. When it was not standing by helplessly, the Punjab Boundary Force actually added to the carnage.[49] In this instance, Hodson's account is unreliable as it almost doubles the Force's actual strength.[50] Lord Mountbatten, aware that the collapse of law and order would be used by opponents as a stick to beat the British, at the time sought to skirt round its ineffectiveness. Despite his misgivings, senior Indian and Pakistani politicians agreed that the Punjab Boundary Force should be wound up at a Joint Defence Council meeting at Lahore on 29 August. No sophistry could hide its abject failure to safeguard the minorities during its 32 day operational existence.

The debate over Lord Mountbatten's handling of security arrangements as over the acceleration of the British withdrawal has, however, obscured the wider issue. The problem of order was in essence not amenable to a military solution in August 1947. This was demonstrated by the fact that although the Indian and Pakistani military evacuation organisations which replaced Major General Rees' force were more effective, the rate of killings actually intensified in the succeeding weeks.

III

The second major set of controversies regarding the Mountbatten Viceroyalty concerns its alleged pro-Congress and hence anti-Pakistan bias. Roberts personalises this by contrasting Mountbatten's differing relations with Nehru and Jinnah. He lists a string of uncomplimentary epithets which found their way into descriptions of the Viceroy's talks with the Muslim League leader.[51] It is undeniable that Lord Mountbatten felt not only less socially at ease with Jinnah, but regarded him as obstructive. He was especially exasperated by Jinnah's determination to become the Governor General of Pakistan.[52] This threw out his existing timetable on the issue of the states' accession as it would not now fall under the purview of a Governor General common to both Dominions.[53] In fairness it should be clarified that Jinnah's announcement on 2 July that he wished to be Governor General was based not on his own vanity, but because he mistrusted both the Congress and Mountbatten and wished further to underline Pakistan's sovereignty by assuming this role.

Alan Campbell-Johnson in a recent conversation with this author cautioned against jumping to the conclusion that Mountbatten's poor personal relations with Jinnah worked against the Muslim League's or later Pakistan's interests. On the contrary he maintained this gave added encouragement for the avoidance of any possible hint of bias in the Viceroy's dealings. Is such a sentiment merely apologetic or does it carry the ring of truth?

The greatest controversies involving Mountbatten's alleged bias have centred around the circumstances of the accession of the Princely State of Kashmir to India and the 'interference' with the Radcliffe Boundary Award in the Punjab region. The former issue is of course related to Lord Mountbatten's role as India's Governor General rather than Viceroy. But it must be mentioned here, as it is linked with the contentious boundary debates. Both over Kashmir and the boundary demarcation, British scholars have recently resurrected criticisms which emanated from Pakistani sources. Alastair Lamb has hammered away at the argument that Mountbatten was 'predisposed' to go along with Nehru's and Patel's 'favoured solutions' in the early phases of the Kashmir crisis.[54] He speculates that Mountbatten secured Hari Singh's signature on the blank Instrument of Accession form on 27 October, i.e. after rather than before as Commander-in-Chief he had acted on Nehru's advice to airlift Indian troops to Srinagar to repel the invading Pakhtun tribesmen. Lamb's assessments are based on circumstantial rather than documentary evidence and in the absence of key sources thus remain open to debate.

A similar situation prevails with regard to the Boundary Awards of the commission chaired by Sir Cyril Radcliffe.[55] There are no records of key events such as the secretary to the Commission, Christopher Beaumont's 'missed lunch' on 12 August, or of the Bikaner State Premier and Chief Engineer's alleged 'meeting' with the Viceroy the preceding day, both of which have been cited as evidence that Mountbatten influenced Radcliffe to amend the boundary in the Ferozepore district in India's favour. There can in any case never be a resolution of the claims and counter-claims beyond a shadow of doubt as Radcliffe destroyed all his papers relating to the Boundary Commission.

Before discussing Christopher Beaumont's widely publicised fresh evidence in the controversy, it is necessary to trace the earlier development of the claims that Mountbatten influenced the determination of the new international boundary which ran through the Punjab. They originated when Sir Francis Mudie, who had stayed on as Governor of the Pakistan Punjab province, alerted the Premier, Liaquat Ali Khan, about a letter of 8 August from Sir George Abell (Private Secretary to the Viceroy) to Stuart Abbott, the Secretary of the Punjab Governor, Sir Evan Jenkins. The letter contained a map which had been given to Mudie by Abbott. It showed a boundary line which included the Muslim majority tehsils (sub-districts) of Zira (65% Muslim population) and Ferozepore (55% Muslim population) in Pakistan, although they were subsequently awarded to India. The map was described as 'showing roughly' the proposed boundary award. Its existence became contentious because the changes were substantial and contained strategic consequences.[56] Moreover, although the elimination of the Ferozepore salient was nothing to do with the award to India of the Muslim majority Gurdaspur district, which provided access to Kashmir, it became linked in the Pakistani mind with what was seen as Mountbatten's general lack of impartiality. Further circumstantial evidence of Lord Mountbatten's intervention was provided by the fact that in the period after 8 August, the Viceroy had received representations from his close friend, the Maharaja of Bikaner, concerning the fate of the neighbouring Ferozepore tehsil which controlled his state's canal headworks. In itself this does not signify anything, as Mountbatten was receiving a number of petitions at this time. Moreover, just because Radcliffe altered his award in a way that was satisfactory to such petitions does not mean that he was prevailed upon by the Viceroy to do so. Radcliffe always maintained that Mountbatten had not sought to influence him. The documentary evidence in the *Transfer of Power* volumes points to Mountbatten steadfastly maintaining a 'hands off' policy towards the boundary awards. He telegrammed the Maharaja of Bikaner on 11 August, for example, declaring that he could not 'intervene or attempt to influence the decision of the Chairman' about the Punjab Boundary award.[57]

Why has such evidence not conclusively resolved the controversy of alleged 'tampering'? The answer lies in the puzzles and discrepancies which have remained in the historical record. John Christie, one of the Viceroy's Assistant Private Secretaries, wrote in his diary for 9 August, for example, that Abell had informed him that Mountbatten 'is in a tired flap and is having to be strenuously dissuaded from asking Radcliffe to alter his awards'.[58] Shahid Hamid, who was private secretary to Field Marshal Sir Claude Auchinleck, in his personal diary published in 1986 noted as an entry for 9 August 1947 that 'Everyone is talking about the impending Boundary Awards ... Many of its salient points have already been leaked out through the staff of the Boundary Commission ... It is common talk that Mountbatten is busy changing it, giving India the Ferozepur headworks ... The Muslims are jittery.'[59]

Especially puzzling is the contradiction between personal recollections of the petitioning on the Ferozepore boundary and that published in the *Transfer of Power*, volume 12. Mountbatten's telegram of 11 August, which has already been referred to above, categorically stated to the Maharaja of Bikaner that: 'I am afraid that I cannot see your Prime Minister and Chief Engineer on this subject (i.e. the award) since I have absolutely nothing to do with the findings of the Boundary Commission.' Shahid Hamid recalls, however, that a 'long interview' did take place between Sardar Panikkar, Bikaner's Prime Minister, and Kanwar Sain, the Chief Engineer, on 11 August.[60] Sain in his memoirs also refers to what must have been an 'off the record' meeting in which the Maharaja's warning was delivered that he would accede to Pakistan if the Ferozepore and Zira tehsils were not awarded to India.[61] The existence of 'off the record' meetings does not in itself prove allegations of the Viceroy's tampering with the Boundary Awards. It highlights, however, the fact that the documentary record might be sanitised and thus cannot remove all doubts about this claim.

Christopher Beaumont's revelations in 1992 gave another twist to the circumstantial evidence relating to Mountbatten's 'alleged' intervention over the Punjab Boundary Award. His claims that Mountbatten, under pressure from Nehru, had persuaded Radcliffe to alter the boundary in India's favour, had been initially raised in a privately distributed paper three years earlier, but had only later been made public with Foreign Office approval. A flurry of letters ensued to the Editor of the *Daily Telegraph* at the end of February 1992. Andrew Roberts' book, published two years later, further publicised the views of Radcliffe's former secretary. Alan Campbell-Johnson has, however, dismissed as mere speculation, Beaumont's claim that his exclusion from a lunch on 12 August between Radcliffe and Ismay, the chief of the Viceroy's staff, provided the opportunity for the Boundary Commission Chairman to be 'overborne'. Nevertheless the fresh doubts cast on Lord Mountbatten's impartiality concerning the boundary demarcation have not been completely dispelled.

The focus on the Viceroy's personal role in boundary demarcation and on his differing relations with Jinnah and Nehru once again obscures wider issues. First and foremost, it is important to acknowledge that, regardless of personalities, there was an increasing convergence of interests between the British and the Congress during 1946-7. Both parties wanted a smooth transition to independence and to avoid a balkanisation of the Subcontinent for strategic and economic reasons. While the British were content to hide behind Jinnah's skirts during the war years, once the hostilities had ceased, the Muslim League was seen as standing in the way of a wider settlement. Unfortunately from both the British and Congress perspective, the League could not be ignored following Jinnah's wartime rise in status and its 1946 electoral success. In these circumstances any British Viceroy would have regarded Jinnah as obstructive and have shared a closer community of interests with Nehru, even if he had not possessed Mountbatten's personal rapport with the Congress leader.

A second important point to note is the continuity between the Wavell and Mountbatten Viceroyalties with respect to the influence wielded by V.P.Menon as Reforms Commissioner. Those who have accused Mountbatten of partiality towards Congress and have claimed that Jinnah was kept more in the dark than Nehru concerning key developments have linked this with Menon's influence and his close ties with such Congress leaders as Patel. Menon, however, was influential not only with respect to the 3 June Partition Plan, but in the drafting of earlier memoranda on the Pakistan proposal during Wavell's Viceroyalty. Thus on 23 January 1946, along with B.N.Rau,[62] he drafted a note on the demarcation of Pakistan which such scholars as Z.H.Zaidi[63] have claimed helped pave the way for the future inclusion of the Gurdaspur district in India. Menon suggested that boundary demarcation in the Punjab should follow a divisional basis with the exception of the Amritsar and Gurdaspur districts of the Lahore division. Amritsar was excluded on the grounds that it was sacred to the Sikhs. He also lumped Gurdaspur with it, neither acknowledging its Muslim majority, nor clarifying what the Sikh objections would be if this district was included in Pakistan. One does not have to link Menon's actions to a conspiracy thesis around the need for Indian access to Kashmir to realise how dependent the British were on what might not have been disinterested advice. Indeed, within two months of the note's production, Abell was warning, 'Mr Menon is now genuinely convinced of the rightness of the Congress view on the general political position. I am convinced that it is not possible to take him into confidence as fully as has been done in the past.'[64]

Muslim civil servants similarly sided with their future masters in the closing months of British rule. The Punjab Governor, Evan Jenkins, for example had the disquieting experience of having his telephone tapped and confidential information passed on to Muslim League politicians.[65] What was significantly different was the fact that there were few Muslim high ranking officials at the centre where the key decisions were being made.

IV

A number of important conclusions stems from this examination of the major themes and controversies surrounding the Mountbatten Viceroyalty. It is evident that, given the absence of key documents, conflicting views will persist relating to the boundary demarcation and accession of the states. The debates remain as politically motivated today as they were for contemporaries. This emphasis on Lord Mountbatten's personal role, whether for exoneration or condemnation, has, however, obfuscated the historical continuities with Wavell's tenure of office. Most importantly it has encouraged an under-estimation of the imperatives which faced his successor. Debate has thus centred around the consequences for good or ill of the advancing of the date of the British departure, rather than on the circumstances out of which this emerged. It was in reality not Lord Mountbatten who accelerated the transfer of power, but the deteriorating law and order situation and the Congress's response to this. Apologists who seek to play down the number of victims of communal massacres, or to inflate the size of the Punjab Boundary Force and its effectiveness, miss this crucial point. Nothing more could have been realistically achieved given the draining of power from British hands and the concerted manipulation of communal hatred. No individual could be held responsible for the massacres, nor could they be attributed to a single act of misjudgement on the British side.

Ironically Lord Mountbatten's achievements as Viceroy have suffered from his own attempts to secure a place in history. By encouraging such writers as Collins and Lapierre to exaggerate his ability to control events, he fell into the trap of critics who wanted a scapegoat for the traumas of August-November 1947 and their subsequent legacy for Indo-Pakistan relations. Lord Mountbatten was in fact as much a helpless bystander of events as a shaper of historical destinies. His plenipotentiary powers were as much a myth as the transfer of power itself. Did the British have any real power to transfer in August 1947? The British knew full well that their time was up in India. The truth is that the end of the Raj was more an exercise in smoke and mirrors than a genuine demission of power. By August 1947 power did not even lie in the key boundary areas of North-West India with the Congress and Muslim League high commands. It had devolved upon local leaders whose murderous intentions were to issue forth with tragic results.

Lord Mountbatten succeeded brilliantly in adding lustre to what could have appeared a humiliating retreat, while at the same time securing Britain's future economic and strategic interests in the Subcontinent and India's membership of the Commonwealth. This was the best that he could achieve in the straitened circumstances of his Viceroyalty. Admirers and critics alike obscure this reality when they depict him as singlehandedly controlling the fate of millions, as the sun finally set on what had been the modern world's greatest empire.

References

1   P. Ziegler *Mountbatten: the official biography* (London, 1985).

2   L.H.Ismay, 1st Baron Ismay *The memoirs of Lord Ismay* (London, 1960).

3   H.V.Hodson *The great divide: Britain-India-Pakistan* (London, 1969).

4   W.H.Morris-Jones, 'The Transfer of Power, 1947: a view from the sidelines' *Modern Asian Studies* 16 (1982) pp. 1-32.

5   A.Campbell-Johnson *Mission with Mountbatten* (London, 1985).

6   R.J.Moore *Escape from Empire: the Attlee Government and the Indian problem* (Oxford, 1983).

7   L.Collins and D.Lapierre *Freedom at Midnight* (London, 1975).

8   Chaudhri Muhammad Ali *The emergence of Pakistan* (New York, 1967).

9   M.A.H.Ispahani *Qaid-e-Azam as I knew him* (Karachi, 1967).

10   Latif Ahmed Sherwani *The Partition of India and Mountbatten* (Karachi, 1986).

11   Y.Krishan, 'Mountbatten and the Partition of India' *History* 68 (1983) pp. 22-38.

12   Bipin Chandra *India's struggle for independence* (New Delhi, 1989).

13   L.Mosley *The last days of the British Raj* (London, 1961).

14   A.Lamb *Kashmir: a disputed legacy 1848-1990* (Hertingfordbury, 1991).

15   A.Roberts *Eminent Churchillians* (London, 1994) pp. 55-136.

16   A.Jalal *The sole spokesman: Jinnah, the Muslim League and the demand for Pakistan* (Cambridge, 1985).

17   See for example, *Locality, province and nation: essays on Indian politics, 1870-1940* eds. J.Gallagher, G.Johnsaon and A.Seal (Cambridge, 1973).

18   Between 1940 and 1946, the number of ICS officials fell from 1,201 to 939; by the latter date, just 429 were British. For a detailed study of the loss of British administrative control, see S.Epstein, 'District Officers in decline: the erosion of British authority in the Bombay countryside 1919-1947' *Modern Asian Studies* 16 (1982) pp. 493-518.

19   For details, see B. Pavier *The Telengana movement 1944-51* (New Delhi, 1981).

20   S.Banerjee *The R.I.N. strike* (New Delhi, 1981).

21   S.Sarkar, 'Popular Movements and National Leadership 1945-47', *Economic and Political Weekly* 17, numbers 14-16 (Apr 1982); S.Sarkar *Modern India 1885-1947* (New Delhi, 1985).

22   I.Talbot *Freedom's cry. The popular dimension in the Pakistan Movement and Partition experience in North-West India* (Karachi, 1996).

23   The Muslim League produced a detailed report on the disturbances which began on 27 October. This was compiled by leading figures from the Punjab and Bengal. See Khwaja Nazimuddin et al. *Report on disturbances in Bihar & UP* (Muslim Information Centre, 1946), IOLR P/T 3363.

24   *Wavell: the Viceroy's journal* ed. P.Moon (London, 1973) p. 370.

25   *Wavell: the Viceroy's journal*, p. 368.

26   *Wavell: the Viceroy's journal*, p. 417.

27   L.F.Mountbatten, 1st Earl Mountbatten *Reflections on the Transfer of Power and Jawaharlal Nehru* (The Second Jawaharlal Nehru Memorial Lecture, London, 1968) p. 6.

28   For details, see I.Talbot, 'Mountbatten and the Partition of India: a rejoinder' *History* 69 (1984) p. 30 and ff.

29   *Transfer of Power*, x, p. 282: Note by Sir Evan Jenkins, 16 Apr 1947.

30   Its 'Conclusions' are reproduced as Appendix II in Hodson, *The great divide*.

31   'Lord Mountbatten on his Viceroyalty' *Asiatic Review* 44 (Oct 1948).

32   Collins and Lapierre, *Freedom at Midnight*, pp. 165-6.

33   *Transfer of Power*, x, pp. 419-23: Note on the partition of the armed forces, 25 Apr 1947.

34   Krishan, 'Mountbatten and the Partition of India', p. 26.

35   See, for example, Chandra, *India's struggle*, pp. 498-9.

36   R.Hough *Mountbatten: hero of our times* (London, 1980) pp. 218, 225.

37   Roberts, *Eminent Churchillians*, p. 90.

38   Roberts, *Eminent Churchillians*, p. 89.

39   Roberts, *Eminent Churchillians*, p. 90.

40   Chandra, *India's struggle*, p. 499.

41   Roberts, *Eminent Churchillians*, p. 89.

42   Roberts, *Eminent Churchillians*, p. 111.

43   IOLR L/P&J/5/250, Punjab Fortnightly Reports, 30 Jul 1947 and 13 Aug 1947.

44   IOLR R/3/1/91, Report by John Eustace, Deputy Commissioner, Lahore n.d.

45   During the first week of March, 4,000 shops and businesses were burned down within the walled area of the city: *Civil and Military Gazette* (Lahore) 16 Mar 1947.

46   IOLR R/3/1/91, Jenkins to Mountbatten, 13 Aug 1947.

47   The number of deaths has itself been controversial. The figure of 200,000, cited by P.Moon in *Divide and quit* (London, 1962), has received support from Ziegler and Alan Campbell-Johnson. The latter claims the massacres were of short duration, but Indian newspapers carry reports of violence as late as November in the Punjab region. Trouble continued in Ajmer until the end of that month, while riots in Karachi in January 1948 led to a belated departure of over 11,000 Hindus from that city. The final figure for the massacres will never be known: the estimate of a death toll of half a million by Gopal Das Khosla *Stern reckoning; a survey of events leading up to and following the Partition of India* (New Delhi, 1989) is likely to

be nearer the truth than Moon's figure. It is a great pity that the issue of the number of fatalities has become something of a political football between Mountbatten's supporters and his critics. This has obfuscated an issue which in any case would have been difficult to corroborate.

48   R.Jeffrey, 'The Punjab Boundary Force and the problem of order, August 1947' *Modern Asian Studies* 8 (1974) pp. 491-520.

49   IOLR R/3/1/173, M.K.Sinha, Report of the Deputy Director, Intelligence Bureau, n.d.

50   The Boundary Force never numbered more than 23,000 troops. Hodson, *Great divide*, p. 344, states, however, that it comprised 55,000 officers and men.

51   These included 'clot', 'evil genius', 'bastard' and 'psychopathic case': Roberts, *Eminent Churchillians*, p. 82.

52   For further details, see A.Jalal, 'Inheriting the Raj: Jinnah and the Governor-Generalship issue' *Modern Asian Studies* 19 (1985) pp. 29-53.

53   R.J.Moore, 'The Mountbatten Viceroyalty' *Journal of Commonwealth and Comparative Politics* 22 (1984) p. 210.

54   Lamb, *Kashmir*, p. 140.

55   The Bengal-Assam and Punjab commissions each had two Congress and two Muslim League nominated High Court judges. The awards were made on Sir Cyril Radcliffe's decision as agreement could not be reached. The boundaries were demarcated on the basis of ascertaining contiguous Muslim and non-Muslim majority areas and 'other factors'. These were not specified thereby opening the way for controversy and raising expectations, as for example the Sikh hope that the holy shrine of Nankana Sahib would be included in India, although it was in a Muslim majority district. For detailed studies and compilations of the Boundary Commission's records, see K.Singh *Partition of Punjab* (Patiala, 1972); *Select documents on Partition of Punjab 1947: India and Pakistan: Punjab, Haryana, and Himachal - India and Punjab - Pakistan* ed. K.Singh (Delhi, 1991); *The Partition of the Punjab 1947: a compilation of official documents* ed. Mian Muhammad Sadullah (9 vols., Lahore, 1983).

56   Ferozepore housed an important Indian Army arsenal.

57   *Transfer of Power*, xii, p. 662: Mountbatten to Bikaner, telegram, 11 Aug 1947.

58   Cited in Ziegler, *Mountbatten*, p. 421, and Moore, 'The Mountbatten Viceroyalty', p. 212.

59   Shahid Hamid *Disastrous twilight: a personal record of the Partition of India* (London, 1986) p. 222.

60   *Transfer of Power*, xii, p. 662.

61   Hamid, *Disastrous twilight*, p. 235.

62   Kanwar Sain *Reminiscences of an engineer* (New Delhi, 1978) pp. 117-24.
63   He later became the chief Indian delegate to the United Nations and was responsible for the drafting and preparation of the Indian constitution.
64   *Jinnah papers*, 1st Series, ii, p. xix and ff.
65   *Transfer of Power*, x, pp. 26-7: Note by Abell, 26 Mar 1947.
66   IOLR L/P&J/5/250, Punjab Fortnightly Report, 14 Mar 1947.